CAMBRIDGE / SCHOOL
Shakespeare

Much Ado About Nothing

Edited by Mary Berry and Michael Clamp

Series Editor: Rex Gibson
Director, Shakespeare and Schools Project

CAMBRIDGE
UNIVERSITY PRESS

PUBLISHED BY THE PRESS SYNDICATE OF THE UNIVERSITY OF CAMBRIDGE
The Pitt Building, Trumpington Street, Cambridge, United Kingdom

CAMBRIDGE UNIVERSITY PRESS
The Edinburgh Building, Cambridge CB2 2RU, UK
40 West 20th Street, New York, NY 10011–4211, USA
477 Williamstown Road, Port Melbourne, VIC 3207, Australia
Ruiz de Alarcón 13, 28014 Madrid, Spain
Dock House, The Waterfront, Cape Town 8001, South Africa

http://www.cambridge.org

First published 1992
Thirteenth printing 2003

Printed and bound by William Clowes Limited, Beccles and London.

A catalogue record for this book is available from the British Library

Library of Congress Cataloguing in Publication data applied for

ISBN 0 521 42610 3 paperback

Designed by Richard Morris, Stonesfield Design
Illustrations by Debbie Abrahams
Picture research by Callie Kendall

Thanks are due to the following for permission to reproduce photographs:

2, 6, 25, 92, 110, 118, 150, Ivan Kyncl; 32, 96, 108, 126, 175, Chris Davies; 46, 58, 80, 102,
Shakespeare Centre Library/Joe Cocks Studio Collection; 54, Stuart Morris; 88, The Viscount
Cowdray: photograph by Courtauld Institute of Art; 177, Courtesy of the National Portrait
Gallery, London; 170, Chris Davies/print by Shakespeare Centre Library; 174, Zöe Dominic;
179, by kind permisson of The Trustees of The Newdegate Settlement/photo courtesy of the
Royal Academy of Arts

Contents

Cambridge School Shakespeare

This edition of *Much Ado About Nothing* is part of the *Cambridge School Shakespeare* series. Like every other play in the series, it has been specially prepared to help all students in schools and colleges.

This *Much Ado About Nothing* aims to be different from other editions of the play. It invites you to bring the play to life in your classroom, hall or drama studio through enjoyable activities that will increase your understanding. Actors have created their different interpretations of the play over the centuries. Similarly, you are encouraged to make up your own mind about *Much Ado About Nothing*, rather than having someone else's interpretation handed down to you.

Cambridge School Shakespeare does not offer you a cut-down or simplified version of the play. This is Shakespeare's language, filled with imaginative possibilities. You will find on every left-hand page: a summary of the action, an explanation of unfamiliar words, a choice of activities on Shakespeare's language, characters and stories.

Between each act and in the pages at the end of the play, you will find notes, illustrations and activities. These will help to increase your understanding of the whole play.

There are a large number of activities to give you the widest choice to suit your own particular needs. Please don't think you have to do every one. Choose the activities that will help you most.

This edition will be of value to you whether you are studying for an examination, reading for pleasure, or thinking of putting on the play to entertain others. You can work on the activities on your own or in groups. Many of the activities suggest a particular group size, but don't be afraid to make up larger or smaller groups to suit your own purposes.

Although you are invited to treat *Much Ado About Nothing* as a play, you don't need special dramatic or theatrical skills to do the activities. By choosing your activities, and by exploring and experimenting, you can make your own interpretations of Shakespeare's language, characters and stories. Whatever you do, remember that Shakespeare wrote his plays to be acted, watched and enjoyed.

Rex Gibson

This edition of *Much Ado About Nothing* uses the text of the play established by F. H. Mares in *The New Cambridge Shakespeare*.

List of characters

Leonato's Household

SIGNOR LEONATO governor of Messina
SIGNOR ANTONIO his brother
HERO Leonato's only daughter
BEATRICE an orphan, Leonato's niece
MARGARET ⎱
URSULA ⎰ gentlewomen attending on Hero
FRIAR FRANCIS
Musicians, Attendants, Maskers and Wedding Guests

The Military

DON PEDRO Prince of Arragon
DON JOHN his bastard brother
COUNT CLAUDIO of Florence ⎱
SIGNOR BENEDICK of Padua ⎰ companions of Don Pedro
BORACHIO ⎱
CONRADE ⎰ followers of Don John
MESSENGER
BALTHASAR a singer
BOY servant to Benedick

The Town

DOGBERRY Constable of Messina
VERGES Deputy Constable (or Headborough)
SEXTON
GEORGE SEACOAL Senior Watchman
WATCHMAN 1
WATCHMAN 2
Other Watchmen

The play is set in Messina

A messenger arrives with a letter informing Leonato that Don Pedro and his victorious army will shortly arrive in Messina. The messenger reports that Count Claudio has performed great deeds.

A hit! A hit! Beatrice fences with her uncle, Leonato.

1 What kind of play is this? (in groups of about seven)

Shakespeare frequently takes advantage of an audience's initial alertness, suggesting through the language the kind of play that they are about to see. Directors naturally look for ways to highlight these ideas and images.

The lights came up on the 1990 Royal Shakespeare Company production to reveal Beatrice defeating her uncle in a fencing bout, much to the delight of the women watching. Sit in a circle and read through lines 1–118. Talk together about why the director chose to open the play in this way.

---

by this by now
three leagues about nine miles
action battle
sort high rank, nobility
none of name no one well known

equally remembered suitably rewarded
figure appearance
badge show or sign
kind natural

Much Ado About Nothing

ACT i   SCENE i
Messina   Leonato's house

Enter LEONATO, *governor of Messina,* HERO *his daughter and*
BEATRICE *his niece, with a* MESSENGER

LEONATO I learn in this letter, that Don Pedro of Arragon comes this
night to Messina.

MESSENGER He is very near by this, he was not three leagues off when I
left him.

LEONATO How many gentlemen have you lost in this action? 5

MESSENGER But few of any sort, and none of name.

LEONATO A victory is twice itself, when the achiever brings home full
numbers. I find here, that Don Pedro hath bestowed much honour on
a young Florentine called Claudio.

MESSENGER Much deserved on his part, and equally remembered by 10
Don Pedro. He hath borne himself beyond the promise of his age,
doing in the figure of a lamb the feats of a lion. He hath indeed better
bettered expectation than you must expect of me to tell you how.

LEONATO He hath an uncle here in Messina will be very much glad of it.

MESSENGER I have already delivered him letters, and there appears 15
much joy in him, even so much that joy could not show itself modest
enough without a badge of bitterness.

LEONATO Did he break out into tears?

MESSENGER In great measure.

LEONATO A kind overflow of kindness: there are no faces truer than 20
those that are so washed. How much better is it to weep at joy, than to
joy at weeping!

Beatrice questions the messenger about Benedick. She teasingly mocks Benedick while the messenger politely defends his fellow soldier's reputation.

---

1 Fancy speaking (in pairs)

Take it in turns to read aloud the messenger's lines 10–13 several times. Emphasise the balances and contrasts (for example, 'much deserved' is balanced by 'equally remembered'). Listen for the sound patterns he makes with initial consonants (**alliteration**) and with different forms of the same word.

Which of Leonato's remarks suggests that the messenger speaks so elaborately that Leonato cannot quite understand him? Does the governor speak in a similarly ornate manner?

2 Beatrice – a formidable woman (in groups of about six)

Everything Beatrice says in the play marks her out as a keenly intelligent and witty woman. In lines 23–70 the messenger does not know quite what has hit him!

a 'You must not, sir, mistake my niece'
  Three of you take the parts of the messenger, Leonato and Hero. The rest share out Beatrice's lines and sit around the messenger, mocking him and deliberately 'mis-taking' his meaning. You will find many other kinds of 'mistakings' in the play.

b What does Beatrice think of Signor Mountanto?
  First hear how often Beatrice mentions Signor Mountanto. ('Mountanto' was an upward sword-thrust in fencing.) One of you speaks Beatrice's lines. The others shout 'Benedick! Benedick!' whenever Beatrice says a 'Benedick word' (such as 'him, he, Benedick'). Then go through lines 23–70 and list all the 'failings' she says he has. Does she like or dislike him?

---

set . . . bills posted notices
at . . . flight to an archery contest
subscribed signed on behalf of
birdbolt blunt-headed arrow
be meet get even
musty victual stale food

holp helped
trencherman good eater
wits parts of the mind
halting limping
next block latest shape
(see page 176)

BEATRICE I pray you, is Signor Mountanto returned from the wars or no?

MESSENGER I know none of that name, lady, there was none such in the
    army of any sort.   25

LEONATO What is he that you ask for, niece?

HERO My cousin means Signor Benedick of Padua.

MESSENGER O he's returned, and as pleasant as ever he was.

BEATRICE He set up his bills here in Messina, and challenged Cupid at
    the flight: and my uncle's fool, reading the challenge, subscribed for   30
    Cupid, and challenged him at the birdbolt. I pray you, how many hath
    he killed and eaten in these wars? But how many hath he killed? – for
    indeed I promised to eat all of his killing.

LEONATO Faith, niece, you tax Signor Benedick too much, but he'll be
    meet with you, I doubt it not.   35

MESSENGER He hath done good service, lady, in these wars.

BEATRICE You had musty victual, and he hath holp to eat it: he is a very
    valiant trencherman, he hath an excellent stomach.

MESSENGER And a good soldier too, lady.

BEATRICE And a good soldier to a lady, but what is he to a lord?   40

MESSENGER A lord to a lord, a man to a man, stuffed with all honourable
    virtues.

BEATRICE It is so indeed, he is no less than a stuffed man, but for the
    stuffing – well, we are all mortal.   .

LEONATO You must not, sir, mistake my niece: there is a kind of merry   45
    war betwixt Signor Benedick and her: they never meet but there's a
    skirmish of wit between them.

BEATRICE Alas, he gets nothing by that. In our last conflict, four of his
    five wits went halting off, and now is the whole man governed with
    one: so that if he have wit enough to keep himself warm, let him bear it   50
    for a difference between himself and his horse, for it is all the wealth
    that he hath left to be known a reasonable creature. Who is his
    companion now? He hath every month a new sworn brother.

MESSENGER Is't possible?

BEATRICE Very easily possible: he wears his faith but as the fashion of his   55
    hat, it ever changes with the next block.

As Beatrice continues to speak mockingly of Benedick to the messenger, Don Pedro and his followers arrive. Leonato welcomes his royal guest and Beatrice begins to taunt Benedick.

1 The messenger

The messenger's part is over by line 70. In Shakespeare's own theatre the actor would now no doubt count the ticket money, or prepare himself for another role later in the play. If you were playing the messenger, would you be clever or dull, serious or comic? Write the thoughts that go through your mind as you talk to the governor and his niece.

2 The governor welcomes his prince
(in groups of nine or more)

Create your own version of lines 66–88. Decide how best to spark off the exchange between Beatrice and Benedick (in one production it was provoked by Benedick bending down and accidentally prodding Beatrice with his sword). What will you do with Don John, Don Pedro's brother?

Identify the characters in the picture and talk about the society the director has created for this production.

your books your good books	**ere a be** before he is
and he were if he were	**charge** trouble, expense
study library	**have it full** are well answered
squarer brawler, hooligan	**fathers herself** i.e. looks like her
pestilence plague	father
taker one who catches it	**marks** takes any notice of
presently immediately	

MESSENGER I see, lady, the gentleman is not in your books.

BEATRICE No, and he were, I would burn my study. But I pray you, who is his companion? Is there no young squarer now, that will make a voyage with him to the devil?   60

MESSENGER He is most in the company of the right noble Claudio.

BEATRICE O Lord, he will hang upon him like a disease: he is sooner caught than the pestilence, and the taker runs presently mad. God help the noble Claudio, if he hath caught the Benedict. It will cost him a thousand pound ere a be cured.   65

MESSENGER I will hold friends with you, lady.

BEATRICE Do, good friend.

LEONATO You will never run mad, niece.

BEATRICE No, not till a hot January.

MESSENGER Don Pedro is approached.   70

Enter DON PEDRO, CLAUDIO, BENEDICK, BALTHASAR *and* JOHN *the bastard*

DON PEDRO Good Signor Leonato, are you come to meet your trouble? The fashion of the world is to avoid cost, and you encounter it.

LEONATO Never came trouble to my house in the likeness of your grace: for trouble being gone, comfort should remain: but when you depart from me, sorrow abides, and happiness takes his leave.   75

DON PEDRO You embrace your charge too willingly. I think this is your daughter?

LEONATO Her mother hath many times told me so.

BENEDICK Were you in doubt, sir, that you asked her?

LEONATO Signor Benedick, no, for then were you a child.   80

DON PEDRO You have it full, Benedick: we may guess by this, what you are, being a man. Truly, the lady fathers herself: be happy, lady, for you are like an honourable father.

BENEDICK If Signor Leonato be her father, she would not have his head on her shoulders for all Messina, as like him as she is.   85

BEATRICE I wonder that you will still be talking, Signor Benedick, nobody marks you.

BENEDICK What, my dear Lady Disdain! Are you yet living?

Beatrice and Benedick renew their 'merry war', each attempting to score points off the other, each trying to have the last word. Leonato invites Don Pedro and the others to be his guests.

1 Fencing match or tennis match? (in pairs)

Again it is Beatrice who interrupts the men's conversation. This time she takes on Benedick, a much more formidable opponent.

a En garde!

Face each other and read lines 86–107 until you are comfortable with the words. Then try 'throwing' the words and insults back and forth as you speak. Who breaks off hostilities first and who wins this particular bout of the 'merry war'?

b We now take you over to the Centre Court

Write your own version of this 'skirmish of wit'. Start with Benedick making his joke (lines 84–5), but from then on construct your own verbal tennis match using key words or ideas from the script. Each time one of you strikes home, give the score (15–love, 15–all, and so on). For example:

BEATRICE You keep *talking* but nobody's *listening* (15–love)
BENEDICK Oh! Hello Miss *Disdain*! Still *alive* are you? (15–all)
BEATRICE There's no chance of *Disdain dying* while . . .

2 'That is the sum of all'

Don Pedro's remark (lines 108–12) suggests that some other business was being quietly discussed while Beatrice and Benedick were sparring. What might this be?

3 Don John's first words (in groups of three)

A character's first words are often very revealing. What do Don John's first words suggest about him? Does he sound like a villain?

Courtesy . . . presence even courtesy itself would be rude to you
dear happiness great good fortune
humour temperament
scape . . . face escape the fate of getting his face scratched
parrot-teacher chatterer
so . . . continuer were as good at keeping going
jade broken-down vicious horse
be forsworn swear in vain

BEATRICE Is it possible Disdain should die, while she hath such meet
food to feed it, as Signor Benedick? Courtesy itself must convert to   90
Disdain, if you come in her presence.

BENEDICK Then is Courtesy a turn-coat: but it is certain I am loved of all
ladies, only you excepted: and I would I could find in my heart that I
had not a hard heart, for truly I love none.

BEATRICE A dear happiness to women, they would else have been   95
troubled with a pernicious suitor. I thank God and my cold blood, I
am of your humour for that: I had rather hear my dog bark at a crow
than a man swear he loves me.

BENEDICK God keep your ladyship still in that mind, so some gentleman
or other shall scape a predestinate scratched face.   100

BEATRICE Scratching could not make it worse, and 'twere such a face as
yours were.

BENEDICK Well, you are a rare parrot-teacher.

BEATRICE A bird of my tongue is better than a beast of yours.

BENEDICK I would my horse had the speed of your tongue, and so good a   105
continuer: but keep your way a God's name. I have done.

BEATRICE You always end with a jade's trick: I know you of old.

DON PEDRO That is the sum of all: Leonato, Signor Claudio and Signor
Benedick, my dear friend Leonato, hath invited you all. I tell him we
shall stay here at the least a month, and he heartily prays some   110
occasion may detain us longer: I dare swear he is no hypocrite, but
prays from his heart.

LEONATO If you swear, my lord, you shall not be forsworn. [*To Don John*]
Let me bid you welcome, my lord, being reconciled to the prince your
brother: I owe you all duty.   115

DON JOHN I thank you, I am not of many words, but I thank you.

LEONATO Please it your grace lead on?

DON PEDRO Your hand, Leonato, we will go together.

Exeunt all except Benedick and Claudio

Claudio tells Benedick of his love for Hero and asks Benedick what he thinks of her. Benedick is unimpressed by Hero's charms and quite dismayed that Claudio should be considering marriage.

1 The two friends (in pairs)

Take parts and read aloud lines 119–50. Claudio must be very serious about his new love, while Benedick must tease him and refuse to take things seriously.

Then choose three striking phrases or sentences that each man uses to describe Hero. What does their way of speaking tell you about the two friends? Benedick is often played as being slightly older than Claudio. Does he sound older to you?

2 Benedick's wit (in small groups)

In lines 136–7, Benedick pretends to think that Claudio is mocking him by making impossible remarks (Cupid, the god of love, was blind; Vulcan, the god of fire, was a blacksmith).

- How many other examples of Benedick's agility of mind and love of play-acting can you find on this page? Has he made any genuinely serious remarks since he appeared?

- 'Shall I never see a bachelor of three score again?', says Benedick the woman-hater (lines 147–8). Can you find any clues that suggest he is more susceptible to women than he would care to admit?

3 Much Ado About Noting?

The play's title has a double meaning. 'Nothing' and 'noting' sounded identical in Shakespeare's time. Both Claudio and Benedick talk of 'noting' (observing) Signor Leonato's daughter. You will find that the play is full of 'notings' as well as 'nothings'.

---

noted her not did not study her
modest sweet, virginal
low short
flouting Jack mocking rascal
go in the song match your mood
wear his cap i.e. to hide his
 cuckold's horns (see page 12)

and thou wilt needs if you must
yoke a wooden frame to harness
 pairs of oxen
sigh away Sundays be stuck at
 home with the wife on Sundays

CLAUDIO Benedick, didst thou note the daughter of Signor Leonato?

BENEDICK I noted her not, but I looked on her. 120

CLAUDIO Is she not a modest young lady?

BENEDICK Do you question me as an honest man should do, for my simple true judgement? Or would you have me speak after my custom, as being a professed tyrant to their sex?

CLAUDIO No, I pray thee speak in sober judgement. 125

BENEDICK Why i'faith, methinks she's too low for a high praise, too brown for a fair praise, and too little for a great praise. Only this commendation I can afford her, that were she other than she is, she were unhandsome, and being no other, but as she is – I do not like her. 130

CLAUDIO Thou thinkest I am in sport. I pray thee, tell me truly how thou lik'st her?

BENEDICK Would you buy her, that you enquire after her?

CLAUDIO Can the world buy such a jewel?

BENEDICK Yea, and a case to put it into. But speak you this with a sad 135 brow? Or do you play the flouting Jack, to tell us Cupid is a good hare-finder, and Vulcan a rare carpenter? Come, in what key shall a man take you, to go in the song?

CLAUDIO In mine eye, she is the sweetest lady that ever I looked on.

BENEDICK I can see yet without spectacles, and I see no such matter. 140 There's her cousin, and she were not possessed with a fury, exceeds her as much in beauty as the first of May doth the last of December. But I hope you have no intent to turn husband, have you?

CLAUDIO I would scarce trust myself, though I had sworn the contrary, if Hero would be my wife. 145

BENEDICK Is't come to this? In faith, hath not the world one man, but he will wear his cap with suspicion? Shall I never see a bachelor of three score again? Go to, i'faith, and thou wilt needs thrust thy neck into a yoke, wear the print of it, and sigh away Sundays. Look, Don Pedro is returned to seek you. 150

Don Pedro returns to find out why his friends have stayed behind.
Benedick reveals the secret of Claudio's love for Hero and vows never to
allow himself to be tempted into marriage.

1 Men's talk (in groups of three)

Here are three men who have been through the wars together. They are alone and relaxed. Read lines 151–215, taking a part each. Speak like these young men and react to your friends' remarks. Benedick should be as 'non-serious' as ever. How like today's young men are they, particularly in their talk of love?

2 What do the men find funny?

The Elizabethans loved to show how clever they could be with words, and these men enjoy showing their intelligence by making jokes about everything.

Love, marriage, allegiance, troth, religion These were all very serious matters in Shakespeare's time. Find out where the three men play lightheartedly with these concerns.

Horns and cuckolds A favourite target for the Elizabethans was the cuckold, a man whose wife was unfaithful to him. The cuckold was supposed to grow horns on his forehead, invisible to himself but obvious to everyone else. Hence Benedick's remark about the married man needing to wear a cap (line 147).

Work out how Benedick elaborates on this idea in lines 178–82. Remember, bugles or hunting horns were originally made from actual animal horns; a 'recheat' is a hunting call; 'winded' means blown or played; and a 'baldrick' is a belt.

The cuckold may have been a male figure of fun, but what does this conversation suggest to you about Elizabethan attitudes to women?

---

allegiance duty to your lord
your . . . part the question your
  lordship is supposed to ask
fetch me in trick me
troth honour, truth, faith
worthy estimable, of high status

die . . . stake be burnt at the stake
  for my beliefs
the despite of your contempt for
maintain . . . will keep up his
  pretence (of being a woman-hater)
  except by will-power
fine conclusion

Enter DON PEDRO

DON PEDRO What secret hath held you here, that you followed not to
Leonato's?

BENEDICK I would your grace would constrain me to tell.

DON PEDRO I charge thee on thy allegiance.

BENEDICK You hear, Count Claudio, I can be secret as a dumb man – I   155
would have you think so. But on my allegiance (mark you this, on my
allegiance) he is in love. With who? Now that is your grace's part:
mark how short his answer is. With Hero, Leonato's short daughter.

CLAUDIO If this were so, so were it uttered.

BENEDICK Like the old tale, my lord: 'It is not so, nor 'twas not so, but   160
indeed, God forbid it should be so.'

CLAUDIO If my passion change not shortly, God forbid it should be
otherwise.

DON PEDRO Amen, if you love her, for the lady is very well worthy.

CLAUDIO You speak this to fetch me in, my lord.   165

DON PEDRO By my troth, I speak my thought.

CLAUDIO And in faith, my lord, I spoke mine.

BENEDICK And by my two faiths and troths, my lord, I spoke mine.

CLAUDIO That I love her, I feel.

DON PEDRO That she is worthy, I know.   170

BENEDICK That I neither feel how she should be loved, nor know how
she should be worthy, is the opinion that fire cannot melt out of me: I
will die in it at the stake.

DON PEDRO Thou wast ever an obstinate heretic in the despite of beauty.

CLAUDIO And never could maintain his part, but in the force of his   175
will.

BENEDICK That a woman conceived me, I thank her: that she brought
me up, I likewise give her most humble thanks: but that I will have a
recheat winded in my forehead, or hang my bugle in an invisible
baldrick, all women shall pardon me. Because I will not do them the   180
wrong to mistrust any, I will do myself the right to trust none: and the
fine is (for the which I may go the finer) I will live a bachelor.

Don Pedro predicts that Benedick, too, will one day fall in love.
Benedick says they have his permission to do all manner of things to ridicule
him if he does.

1 'Benedick the married man' (in small groups)

Draw pictures of the three things that Benedick promises they may do
to him if he falls in love (lines 184–99). Share your ideas with the
group. Many people joke about things that disturb or worry them. Is
Benedick genuinely antagonistic to women, or is it merely a pretence?

2 Show the joke (in groups of three)

Much Elizabethan humour depends on knowledge now lost to a
modern audience. Benedick says 'so I commit you . . .', which was
also an Elizabethan way of ending a letter. Claudio and Don Pedro
pick up Benedick's words and answer in letter-style.

Where possible, actors bring this humour to life with gestures,
expressions and stage 'busyness'. Take a part each and memorise
lines 205–12 (from 'good Signor Benedick' to 'Nay, mock not, mock
not'). Devise a presentation which makes the letter joke clear to the
audience. Show it to the rest of the class and try to make them laugh!

3 Fashions and outward show

Benedick is not going to leave without having the last word. He says
that his friends' mocking use of conventional letter endings ('ere you
flout old ends any further') resembles the trimmings ('guards') which
have been only loosely sewn ('basted') onto the body of a garment.

Benedick is joking here, but costume and dress will assume a
serious and almost tragic importance in future events. Many characters will adopt masks and disguises, many will attempt to judge a
person's inner worth by their outward show.

---

lose . . . love sighing consumed
blood, drinking replenished it
sign . . . Cupid brothel sign
fall . . . faith change your beliefs
argument subject for discussion
bottle wicker basket

Adam a famous archer of the day
as time shall try time will tell
horn-mad raving mad
Venice noted for loose morals
temporise . . . hours change with
time
tuition protection

DON PEDRO I shall see thee, ere I die, look pale with love.

BENEDICK With anger, with sickness, or with hunger, my lord, not
with love: prove that ever I lose more blood with love than I will get   185
again with drinking, pick out mine eyes with a ballad-maker's pen,
and hang me up at the door of a brothel house for the sign of blind
Cupid.

DON PEDRO Well, if ever thou dost fall from this faith, thou wilt prove a
notable argument.   190

BENEDICK If I do, hang me in a bottle like a cat, and shoot at me, and he
that hits me, let him be clapped on the shoulder, and called Adam.

DON PEDRO Well, as time shall try: 'In time the savage bull doth bear the
yoke.'

BENEDICK The savage bull may, but if ever the sensible Benedick bear it,   195
pluck off the bull's horns, and set them in my forehead, and let me be
vilely painted, and in such great letters as they write, 'Here is good
horse to hire', let them signify under my sign, 'Here you may see
Benedick the married man.'

CLAUDIO If this should ever happen, thou wouldst be horn-mad.   200

DON PEDRO Nay, if Cupid have not spent all his quiver in Venice, thou
wilt quake for this shortly.

BENEDICK I look for an earthquake too then.

DON PEDRO Well, you will temporise with the hours. In the mean time,
good Signor Benedick, repair to Leonato's, commend me to him, and   205
tell him I will not fail him at supper, for indeed he hath made great
preparation.

BENEDICK I have almost matter enough in me for such an embassage,
and so I commit you –

CLAUDIO To the tuition of God: from my house if I had it –   210

DON PEDRO The sixth of July: your loving friend Benedick.

BENEDICK Nay, mock not, mock not: the body of your discourse is
sometime guarded with fragments, and the guards are but slightly
basted on, neither: ere you flout old ends any further, examine your
conscience: and so I leave you.   *Exit*   215

*Claudio tells how his love for Hero has grown since his return from the war.
The prince offers to woo Hero on his friend's behalf. That night at the
masked ball he will pretend to be Claudio.*

1 The soldier and the lover (in large groups)

In lines 223–31 Claudio tells Don Pedro that he saw and liked Hero
before they set off on their campaign, but thoughts of war were too
pressing to allow thoughts of love to grow. Now the war is over,
Hero's charms cannot be denied.

- Find out how words about love and war echo through their
  language. Two of you take the parts of Claudio and Don Pedro and
  read slowly lines 224–54. The rest divide into two groups. One
  group listens for and repeats all the 'soft/love' words. The other
  group listens for and echoes all the 'rough/war' words. Decide
  where the two groups of words coincide. Can you suggest why?

- How genuine is Claudio? You may have found many 'soft/love'
  words in his conversation with Don Pedro. Does Claudio say
  anything which suggests that his interest is not solely confined to
  Hero's beauty and charm?

2 From prose to blank verse (in pairs)

Up to the departure of Benedick, the play has been in prose. Now
Claudio and Don Pedro begin to speak in blank (unrhymed) verse.
Take a part each, sit face to face and read lines 216–54. Compare the
way the two men speak here with the way they have just been talking
to Benedick (pages 184–5 will help you with the different structures
of prose and blank verse if needed).

---

apt eager, quick
affect care for
break broach the subject
his complexion its appearance
salved it expressed it more gently
treatise account, explanation

What need . . . flood? a bridge
 need only be as broad as the river
The fairest . . . necessity the best
 gift is one that meets the need
Look what whatever
'tis once in a word
fit thee provide you

CLAUDIO My liege, your highness now may do me good.

DON PEDRO My love is thine to teach, teach it but how,
        And thou shalt see how apt it is to learn
        Any hard lesson that may do thee good.

CLAUDIO Hath Leonato any son, my lord?   220

DON PEDRO No child but Hero, she's his only heir:
        Dost thou affect her, Claudio?

CLAUDIO   O my lord,
        When you went onward on this ended action,
        I looked upon her with a soldier's eye,
        That liked, but had a rougher task in hand,   225
        Than to drive liking to the name of love;
        But now I am returned, and that war-thoughts
        Have left their places vacant, in their rooms
        Come thronging soft and delicate desires,
        All prompting me how fair young Hero is,   230
        Saying I liked her ere I went to wars.

DON PEDRO Thou wilt be like a lover presently,
        And tire the hearer with a book of words:
        If thou dost love fair Hero, cherish it,
        And I will break with her, and with her father,   235
        And thou shalt have her. Wast not to this end,
        That thou began'st to twist so fine a story?

CLAUDIO How sweetly you do minister to love,
        That know love's grief by his complexion!
        But lest my liking might too sudden seem,   240
        I would have salved it with a longer treatise.

DON PEDRO What need the bridge much broader than the flood?
        The fairest grant is the necessity.
        Look what will serve is fit: 'tis once, thou lovest,
        And I will fit thee with the remedy.   245
        I know we shall have revelling tonight,
        I will assume thy part in some disguise,
        And tell fair Hero I am Claudio,
        And in her bosom I'll unclasp my heart,
        And take her hearing prisoner with the force   250
        And strong encounter of my amorous tale:
        Then after, to her father will I break,
        And the conclusion is, she shall be thine:
        In practice let us put it presently.

                                            Exeunt

Antonio tells Leonato that Don Pedro's conversation with Claudio has been overheard. Apparently, Don Pedro is in love with Hero and intends to propose marriage that evening at the masked ball.

1 Judging by appearances (in pairs)

This scene between Leonato and his brother tells us of the first of many eavesdroppings, mistaken conclusions and misreportings in the play. Read the scene through taking a part each.

- Talk about how you would suggest the two actors should play this scene so as to create a sense of gossip and rumour.
- How accurately has the servant 'noted' the conversation between Don Pedro and Claudio? Which brother seems more inclined to believe the servant's story?
- Find two phrases which specifically refer to outward appearances. How many similar examples can you find in the opening lines of the play (1.1.1–22)?

2 Prepare for the supper (in small groups)

The scene ends with great hustle and bustle as Leonato and his household get ready for the banquet and dancing.

Show your group's version of lines 13–21 to the rest of the class. Two of you take the named parts, the rest help to create an atmosphere of domestic activity. It will go much more smoothly if Leonato learns his lines.

3 'I will acquaint my daughter withal'

Compare the merits of Don Pedro and Claudio as prospective husbands. Has Hero said or done anything so far to give you a clue as to her preferred choice? Which man might Leonato favour?

How now Hello, what news?
cousin kinsman
As the events stamps them it
  depends on the outcome
cover outward appearance
thick-pleached hedged, wooded
discovered revealed

accordant in agreement
take . . . top seize the opportunity
break . . . it discuss it with you
appear itself actually happens
peradventure perhaps
cry you mercy beg your pardon

ACT 1   SCENE 2
Leonato's house

Enter LEONATO *and an old man* ANTONIO, *brother to Leonato*

LEONATO How now, brother, where is my cousin your son? Hath he
provided this music?

ANTONIO He is very busy about it: but, brother, I can tell you strange
news that you yet dreamed not of.

LEONATO Are they good?   5

ANTONIO As the events stamps them, but they have a good cover: they
show well outward. The prince and Count Claudio walking in a
thick-pleached alley in mine orchard, were thus much overheard by a
man of mine: the prince discovered to Claudio that he loved my niece
your daughter, and meant to acknowledge it this night in a dance, and   10
if he found her accordant, he meant to take the present time by the
top, and instantly break with you of it.

LEONATO Hath the fellow any wit that told you this?

ANTONIO A good sharp fellow, I will send for him, and question him
yourself.   15

LEONATO No, no, we will hold it as a dream till it appear itself: but I will
acquaint my daughter withal, that she may be the better prepared for
an answer, if peradventure this be true: go you, and tell her of it.
[Several persons cross the stage]
Cousins, you know what you have to do. O I cry you mercy, friend, go
you with me and I will use your skill: good cousin, have a care this   20
busy time.
Exeunt

Don John has chosen not to attend the supper. He tells Conrade of his extreme discontent. Conrade urges him to avoid causing further trouble, but Don John's bitter anger will not be softened.

1 The 'plain-dealing villain' (in groups of three)

The first stage direction describes Don John as 'the bastard'. In Shakespeare's day, a person born outside marriage was expected to be jealous, scheming and bad-tempered (see page 166). Take a part each and read the whole scene.

- What part has 'the bastard' played in the recent war and why is he so resentful of his brother and of Claudio?

- Don John says (lines 8–10) that Conrade, born under the planet Saturn, should be sour and gloomy like himself. Do you think Conrade is like this?

- Don John's 'thought-lists'. Read aloud lines 8–13 and 20–7, handing over to the next person at the end of each thought (generally marked by a full stop or colon). Emphasise the patterns in Don John's words. What sort of villain does he sound like?

2 A change of mood (in groups of four)

On Shakespeare's stage the action probably flowed quickly from scene to scene. Indeed, the earliest published versions of his plays did not divide the script into separate acts or scenes at all.

Two of you play Leonato and Antonio, the other two play Don John and Conrade. Rehearse your version of the final few lines of Scene 2 together with the first few lines of Scene 3. Make the action flow without a break, but emphasise the change of atmosphere. Present your version to the rest of the class.

What . . . year What the devil!
out of measure excessively
moral medicine words of advice
mortifying mischief fatal disease
claw flatter

stood out rebelled
frame bring about
canker wild rose
fashion a carriage put on an act
clog heavy wooden block (used to tether animals)

ACT 1   SCENE 3
Outside Leonato's house

Enter DON JOHN the bastard and CONRADE his companion

CONRADE What the good year, my lord, why are you thus out of measure
sad?

DON JOHN There is no measure in the occasion that breeds, therefore the
sadness is without limit.

CONRADE You should hear reason.   5

DON JOHN And when I have heard it, what blessing brings it?

CONRADE If not a present remedy, at least a patient sufferance.

DON JOHN I wonder that thou (being as thou sayest thou art, born under
Saturn) goest about to apply a moral medicine to a mortifying
mischief. I cannot hide what I am: I must be sad when I have cause,   10
and smile at no man's jests: eat when I have stomach, and wait for no
man's leisure: sleep when I am drowsy, and tend on no man's
business: laugh when I am merry, and claw no man in his humour.

CONRADE Yea, but you must not make the full show of this till you may do
it without controlment. You have of late stood out against your   15
brother, and he hath ta'en you newly into his grace, where it is
impossible you should take true root, but by the fair weather that you
make yourself: it is needful that you frame the season for your own
harvest.

DON JOHN I had rather be a canker in a hedge, than a rose in his grace,   20
and it better fits my blood to be disdained of all, than to fashion a
carriage to rob love from any. In this (though I cannot be said to be a
flattering honest man) it must not be denied but I am a plain-dealing
villain. I am trusted with a muzzle, and enfranchised with a clog,
therefore I have decreed not to sing in my cage. If I had my mouth, I   25
would bite: if I had my liberty, I would do my liking. In the mean time,
let me be that I am, and seek not to alter me.

CONRADE Can you make no use of your discontent?

DON JOHN I make all use of it, for I use it only. Who comes here?

Borachio comes from the banquet and tells of Don Pedro's plan to woo Hero on Claudio's behalf. Don John decides to use this information to get his revenge on Claudio.

1 Borachio (in pairs)

Take a part each and read lines 30–50. Does Borachio speak at all like his sullen and resentful master?

2 Noting and cuckolds again

Borachio is the second person to have eavesdropped on Don Pedro and Claudio. Has he 'noted' things more accurately than Antonio's servant?

'What is he for a fool that betroths himself to unquietness?', says Don John (lines 34–5), meaning 'What kind of fool wishes to get married and give himself nothing but worry?' Which other character has earlier expressed a similar distaste of women and marriage?

3 Show Don John's dearest wish (in large groups)

'Would the cook were a my mind', says Don John as he leaves for the banquet (line 53). Devise a mime version of what Don John dearly wishes to happen at the banquet.

4 What is your picture of Don John?

One production had Don John dressed to look like Napoleon. What would be your choice of costume/make-up? Which actor from film, television or theatre would you choose to play him?

---

for any model as a design
forward March-chick precocious
  youngster
Being . . . perfumer instructed to
  make the rooms sweet-smelling

smoking fumigating
arras wall-hangings
start-up upstart
were a my mind thought like me
go prove go and find out

Enter BORACHIO

What news, Borachio?   30

BORACHIO I came yonder from a great supper, the prince your brother is
royally entertained by Leonato, and I can give you intelligence of an
intended marriage.

DON JOHN Will it serve for any model to build mischief on? What is he for
a fool that betroths himself to unquietness?   35

BORACHIO Marry, it is your brother's right hand.

DON JOHN Who, the most exquisite Claudio?

BORACHIO Even he.

DON JOHN A proper squire! And who, and who, which way looks he?

BORACHIO Marry, on Hero, the daughter and heir of Leonato.   40

DON JOHN A very forward March-chick. How came you to this?

BORACHIO Being entertained for a perfumer, as I was smoking a musty
room, comes me the prince and Claudio, hand in hand, in sad
conference: I whipped me behind the arras, and there heard it agreed
upon, that the prince should woo Hero for himself, and having   45
obtained her, give her to Count Claudio.

DON JOHN Come, come, let us thither, this may prove food to my
displeasure, that young start-up hath all the glory of my overthrow: if I
can cross him any way, I bless myself every way. You are both sure,
and will assist me?   50

CONRADE To the death, my lord.

DON JOHN Let us to the great supper, their cheer is the greater that I am
subdued. Would the cook were a my mind: shall we go prove what's to
be done?

BORACHIO We'll wait upon your lordship.   55

Exeunt

Looking back at Act 1

1 What news? (in groups of five to eight)

The gossip columnist One of you is a gossip columnist. Your sources of information are queuing up to tell you of the latest news and scandal amongst Messina society. The other group members make a list of different pieces of news from Act 1. Each in turn tells the gossip columnist a piece of news. The gossip columnist should cross-examine each of the informants to make sure the details are correct.

The messenger The messenger returns to his regiment and tells his friends about news he carried to Leonato. He then gives them his impressions of Leonato, Hero and Beatrice. As he relates his story, his friends question him about the characters, events and the household he describes.

2 Friends (in groups of three)

Benedick, Don Pedro and Claudio seem to be good friends. They have, after all, just fought together against Don John.

Choose a character each. Make a large outline drawing of your character and inside it write:

- your status in relation to your two friends
- what you have in common with your friends
- the ways in which you are different from your friends
- what binds you together.

Show your drawings to each other and swap your ideas about these three men.

3 Masked and unmasked

When his brother is present, Don John has to mask his ill feeling. However, Shakespeare often gives his villains opportunities to confess their secret thoughts to the audience. Write a monologue for Don John, which he might speak at the end of Act 1 Scene 3 after Borachio and Conrade have left. Write it in the same style of prose that Don John uses earlier in the scene.

4 'A kind of merry war' – or is it?

Here we see Benedick the returning soldier, apparently careless and carefree. But is he?

What does he really think of Beatrice and what are his thoughts after their latest 'skirmish of wit'?

Write two extracts from Benedick's diary: one written that evening and one written after an earlier meeting with Beatrice before he went away to war.

5 Friends, cousins, lovers and haters

Characters in Shakespearean comedy often behave like figures in a dance, forming patterns of relationships which dissolve and re-form as the play progresses. Act 1 is concerned with young people (Claudio, Benedick, Hero and Beatrice) and the seriously enjoyable matters of friendship, falling in love and getting married.

Make notes on the patterns of relationships forming between these four characters. For example, how does the 'love' pair, Claudio and Hero, compare with the 'love–hate' pair, Beatrice and Benedick? How does Beatrice contrast with her cousin Hero and how much alike are Benedick and his friend, Claudio? You may wish to present your findings as a diagram or chart.

6 Leonato expects a visitor

Improvise a scene where a manager is awaiting the arrival of his powerful, important company chairman, whom he has invited for dinner. Like Don Pedro, the chairman is unmarried and, like Leonato, the manager has a young, unmarried daughter. Your improvisation might begin with the manager advising his daughter about how to behave!

After your improvisation, look back at 1.1.71–118. Talk about how you would want Leonato to behave at key points during this dialogue.

After supper, Beatrice describes her ideal man and speaks mockingly of Don John and Benedick. Leonato warns her that such talk will not get her a husband, but Beatrice says she is happy to stay single.

---

1 Family talk (in groups of four)

This scene opens with a private glimpse of the governor's household. How complex are these family relationships? Take a part each (including the silent Hero).

a Conversation or battle?

Read lines 1–60 in two ways: firstly as a relaxed and leisurely family conversation, and then more forcefully as if you are engaged in a battle of wits and opinions.

Which way seems to work better? The silent Hero must give her opinion of what she hears.

b Play the relationship game

Read lines 1–60 together. Think carefully about who says what to whom, then prepare to make statements, in role, to the other three. To each character in turn you must state your name, describe yourself and your relationship to them, give your opinion of them, and finally compare your view of marriage with what you believe is theirs. When you finish speaking to a character, he or she must immediately reply to you in the same way. The pattern could be something as simple as:

'My name is . . . I am an old/young . . . I am your . . . I think you are . . . Marriage is . . .'

but decide on your own format.

2 Cows, apes and bears (in pairs)

Beatrice enjoys conjuring up fantastic word-pictures. Draw your impression of Beatrice as the 'curst' (bad-tempered) cow who is sent short horns so that it can do no damage (see page 185), or the old maid who leads apes into hell. Add captions or speech bubbles.

---

tartly sourly
image statue
if a could if he could
shrewd shrewish, or sharp
lessen . . . sending reduce what God has given me

just just so
at him praying to God
the woollen scratchy blankets
even take just take
in earnest of the bearward as a token payment from the bear-keeper

ACT 2 SCENE 1
The great chamber of Leonato's house

Enter LEONATO, *his brother* ANTONIO, HERO *his daughter and*
BEATRICE *his niece*

LEONATO Was not Count John here at supper?

ANTONIO I saw him not.

BEATRICE How tartly that gentleman looks, I never can see him but I am
heart-burned an hour after.

HERO He is of a very melancholy disposition.   5

BEATRICE He were an excellent man that were made just in the mid-way
between him and Benedick: the one is too like an image and says
nothing, and the other too like my lady's eldest son, evermore tattling.

LEONATO Then half Signor Benedick's tongue in Count John's mouth,
and half Count John's melancholy in Signor Benedick's face –   10

BEATRICE With a good leg and a good foot, uncle, and money enough in
his purse, such a man would win any woman in the world if a could get
her good will.

LEONATO By my troth, niece, thou wilt never get thee a husband, if thou
be so shrewd of thy tongue.   15

ANTONIO In faith, she's too curst.

BEATRICE Too curst is more than curst, I shall lessen God's sending that
way: for it is said, God sends a curst cow short horns, but to a cow too
curst, he sends none.

LEONATO So, by being too curst, God will send you no horns.   20

BEATRICE Just, if he send me no husband, for the which blessing I am at
him upon my knees every morning and evening: Lord, I could not
endure a husband with a beard on his face, I had rather lie in the
woollen!

LEONATO You may light on a husband that hath no beard.   25

BEATRICE What should I do with him – dress him in my apparel and
make him my waiting gentlewoman? He that hath a beard is more
than a youth: and he that hath no beard is less than a man: and he that
is more than a youth, is not for me, and he that is less than a man, I am
not for him: therefore I will even take sixpence in earnest of the   30
bearward, and lead his apes into hell.

27

Beatrice mockingly advises Hero on when and when not to obey her father in the matter of marriage. She then gives her own views of courtship, weddings and the regrets of life after marriage.

1 A not-so-silent Hero (in groups of four)

For Hero this is a very important evening. A prince is to propose marriage. Will she accept? Dare she refuse?

Prepare a presentation of lines 38–57 in which Hero breaks her silence. After each sentence Hero adds her own comment (perhaps agreeing or disagreeing and explaining why).

2 'Wooing, wedding, and repenting' (in pairs)

Beatrice describes courtship and marriage as being like dances. Devise a mime based on lines 52–7 in which you woo, marry and repent in a series of dances:

- a Scotch jig: a lively dance ('hot and hasty')
- a measure: a slow, formal dance ('full of state and ancientry')
- a cinquepace (pronounced 'sink-a-pace'): a capering dance of five steps followed by a leap.

Show your version to the rest of the class or, if there is room, the whole class can dance out their versions together.

3 Double meanings and dirty jokes

Elizabethans would have enjoyed the game of sexual innuendo that Beatrice and Leonato play in lines 11–47. 'Will' could mean lust or the sexual organs, and 'foot' was a Biblical euphemism for the penis. 'Purse', 'horns' and 'fitted' all had bawdy meanings. Would you advise modern actors to try to bring out the bawdiness in this conversation?

Saint Peter guardian of the gates of heaven
metal substance
earth/dust/marl Beatrice plays with the idea that God created Adam, the first man, out of earth

match . . . kindred marry a close relative
in . . . kind i.e. propose marriage
important pushy, hasty
measure (1) moderation (2) dance
the first suit wooing
passing shrewdly very sharply

LEONATO Well then, go you into hell.

BEATRICE No, but to the gate, and there will the devil meet me like an old
cuckold with horns on his head, and say, get you to heaven, Beatrice,
get you to heaven, here's no place for you maids. So deliver I up my   35
apes, and away to Saint Peter: for the heavens, he shows me where the
bachelors sit, and there live we, as merry as the day is long.

ANTONIO Well, niece, I trust you will be ruled by your father.

BEATRICE Yes faith, it is my cousin's duty to make curtsy, and say, father,
as it please you: but yet for all that, cousin, let him be a handsome   40
fellow, or else make another curtsy, and say, father, as it please me.

LEONATO Well, niece, I hope to see you one day fitted with a husband.

BEATRICE Not till God make men of some other metal than earth: would
it not grieve a woman to be overmastered with a piece of valiant dust?
to make an account of her life to a clod of wayward marl? No, uncle,   45
I'll none: Adam's sons are my brethren, and truly I hold it a sin to
match in my kindred.

LEONATO Daughter, remember what I told you: if the prince do solicit
you in that kind, you know your answer.

BEATRICE The fault will be in the music, cousin, if you be not wooed in   50
good time: if the prince be too important, tell him there is measure in
everything, and so dance out the answer. For hear me, Hero, wooing,
wedding, and repenting, is as a Scotch jig, a measure and a
cinquepace: the first suit is hot and hasty like a Scotch jig (and full as
fantastical), the wedding mannerly modest (as a measure) full of state   55
and ancientry, and then comes Repentance, and with his bad legs falls
into the cinquepace faster and faster, till he sink into his grave.

LEONATO Cousin, you apprehend passing shrewdly.

BEATRICE I have a good eye, uncle, I can see a church by daylight.

LEONATO The revellers are entering, brother, make good room.   60

[*Exit Antonio*]

Don Pedro, his friends and attendants enter wearing masks. The room fills with people and the dancing begins. The women mock the men as they dance.

1 Take your partners! (in groups of six)

Masking was a favourite entertainment in great Elizabethan households. A group of masked male dancers would enter the chamber and take partners from the assembled guests.

This masked dance is full of ill-matched couples. In pairs, choose one of the following activities:

a The handsome prince?
Memorise lines 61–70. Hero believes that the masked Don Pedro will declare his love for her. Decide whether she wants him to or not and show her response.

b Give him the brush-off
Memorise lines 71–81. Perhaps Margaret is very fond of another man? Show her resisting the masked Balthasar's advances.

c Youth and age
Memorise lines 82–91. Show Ursula making fun of the masked Antonio. What are the old man's reactions?

Rehearse the three parts in sequence (perhaps with suitable music), as if you were in the middle of a dance, then show it to the rest of the class.

2 Eyeing up the talent (in groups of six)

To get a sense of how the characters might behave here, improvise a scene in a disco. As the music plays, three girls discuss the attributes of the men present, men with similar qualities to Don Pedro, Balthasar and Antonio. Show what happens when the girls are asked for a dance.

---

walk a bout dance
So you so long as you
favour face
God defend . . . case I hope your face looks better than your mask!
visor mask

Philemon's roof . . . Jove . . .
  thatched both are showing off their classical learning (see page 182)
clerk church official who leads the responses to the prayers
up and down all over
Go to, mum Come, say no more

Enter DON PEDRO, CLAUDIO, BENEDICK *and* BALTHASAR, *Maskers with a drum;* [*re-enter* ANTONIO, *masked, followed by*] DON JOHN [*and* BORACHIO *and others including* MARGARET *and* URSULA. *The dance begins*]

DON PEDRO Lady, will you walk a bout with your friend?
HERO So you walk softly, and look sweetly, and say nothing, I am yours for
    the walk, and especially when I walk away.
DON PEDRO With me in your company.
HERO I may say so when I please.   65
DON PEDRO And when please you to say so?
HERO When I like your favour, for God defend the lute should be like the
    case.
DON PEDRO My visor is Philemon's roof, within the house is Jove.
HERO Why then your visor should be thatched.
DON PEDRO   Speak low if you speak love.   70
                [*They move on in the dance*]
[BALTHASAR] Well, I would you did like me.
MARGARET So would not I for your own sake, for I have many ill
    qualities.
[BALTHASAR] Which is one?
MARGARET I say my prayers aloud.   75
[BALTHASAR] I love you the better, the hearers may cry amen.
MARGARET God match me with a good dancer.
BALTHASAR Amen.
MARGARET And God keep him out of my sight when the dance is done:
    answer, clerk.   80
BALTHASAR No more words, the clerk is answered.
                [*They move on in the dance*]
URSULA I know you well enough, you are Signor Antonio.
ANTONIO At a word, I am not.
URSULA I know you by the waggling of your head.
ANTONIO To tell you true, I counterfeit him.   85
URSULA You could never do him so ill-well, unless you were the very
    man: here's his dry hand up and down, you are he, you are he.
ANTONIO At a word, I am not.
URSULA Come, come, do you think I do not know you by your excellent
    wit? Can virtue hide itself? Go to, mum, you are he, graces will   90
    appear, and there's an end.
                [*They move on in the dance*]

*Benedick, thinking his true identity is hidden behind his mask, teases
Beatrice, but she promptly turns the tables on him. Don John tells
Claudio that Don Pedro loves Hero.*

1 Ouch!

Benedick momentarily lifts his mask so we can see how Beatrice's words
have really stung him.

What do you think she has just said to him?

2 Thoughts behind the mask (in groups of four)

Two of you read aloud lines 92–114. Decide when Beatrice pene-
trates Benedick's disguise (or has she already guessed?). Then read
the lines again with the other two cutting in at different moments to
say what their character is thinking. Whose cutting remarks sting the
most?

Hundred ... Tales a joke book
What's he? who's he?
only his gift his only talent
libertines good-for-nothings
villainy offensiveness
angers them i.e. when he makes
  offensive jokes about them

fleet company
but ... comparison just make a
  few clever remarks
partridge wing a small morsel
amorous on in love with
visor masked person

BEATRICE Will you not tell me who told you so?

BENEDICK No, you shall pardon me.

BEATRICE Nor will you not tell me who you are?

BENEDICK Not now.   95

BEATRICE That I was disdainful, and that I had my good wit out of *The Hundred Merry Tales*: well, this was Signor Benedick that said so.

BENEDICK What's he?

BEATRICE I am sure you know him well enough.

BENEDICK Not I, believe me.   100

BEATRICE Did he never make you laugh?

BENEDICK I pray you, what is he?

BEATRICE Why he is the prince's jester, a very dull fool, only his gift is, in devising impossible slanders: none but libertines delight in him, and the commendation is not in his wit, but in his villainy, for he both   105 pleases men and angers them, and then they laugh at him, and beat him: I am sure he is in the fleet, I would he had boarded me.

BENEDICK When I know the gentleman, I'll tell him what you say.

BEATRICE Do, do, he'll but break a comparison or two on me, which peradventure (not marked, or not laughed at) strikes him into   110 melancholy, and then there's a partridge wing saved, for the fool will eat no supper that night. We must follow the leaders.

BENEDICK In every good thing.

BEATRICE Nay, if they lead to any ill, I will leave them at the next turning.

    Music for the Dance. [They Dance.] Exeunt [all but Don John,
                      Borachio and Claudio]

DON JOHN Sure my brother is amorous on Hero, and hath withdrawn her   115 father to break with him about it: the ladies follow her, and but one visor remains.

BORACHIO And that is Claudio, I know him by his bearing.

DON JOHN Are not you Signor Benedick?

CLAUDIO You know me well, I am he.   120

DON JOHN Signor, you are very near my brother in his love, he is enamoured on Hero, I pray you dissuade him from her, she is no equal for his birth: you may do the part of an honest man in it.

CLAUDIO How know you he loves her?

DON JOHN I heard him swear his affection.   125

BORACHIO So did I too, and he swore he would marry her tonight.

DON JOHN Come, let us to the banquet.

                             Exeunt Don John and Borachio

Claudio believes Don John's lie. Benedick also tells him that Don Pedro has won the heart of Hero. The unhappy Claudio creeps away, leaving Benedick smarting at the memory of Beatrice's taunts.

---

1 Claudio reflects on events (in groups of about six)

Claudio reveals his thoughts in blank verse. Read his soliloquy together (lines 128–38), each person handing over to the next person at a colon or full stop. Try it in different ways: quickly and angrily, slowly and resignedly, full of anguish and despair. Decide which way works best and where Claudio places the blame – on Don Pedro or on Hero?

2 Fight like a man (in pairs)

Benedick (lines 143–6) says that Claudio must either:

- give up Hero and wear the willow garland (the badge of the unhappy lover) round his neck like a money-lender's ('usurer's') gold chain

- or be a man, challenge the prince to a fight and wear the willow garland bravely across his chest like a soldier's sash.

Decide which option Claudio chooses, show it in the way he exits, then discuss what you think of this young man who so distinguished himself in the recent war.

3 Benedick reflects on events (in pairs)

Unlike Claudio, Benedick prefers to think in prose. See how he argues with himself (or with the audience?). Sit facing each other and read lines 154–9 aloud together. Change seats at each colon or exclamation mark. Decide how the argument has shifted and show that in your voice. How deeply have Beatrice's words hurt you?

Afterwards, write detailed notes instructing an actor on how best to speak these six lines on stage.

---

faith loyalty (to a friend)
blood passion
accident . . . proof something which is constantly being proved true
mistrusted not did not suspect
county count

drovier cattle drover or dealer
sedges undergrowth
puts . . . person assumes the world thinks as she does
so gives me out causes such things to be said about me

CLAUDIO Thus answer I in name of Benedick,
   But hear these ill news with the ears of Claudio:
   'Tis certain so, the prince woos for himself,   130
   Friendship is constant in all other things,
   Save in the office and affairs of love:
   Therefore all hearts in love use their own tongues.
   Let every eye negotiate for itself,
   And trust no agent: for beauty is a witch,   135
   Against whose charms faith melteth into blood:
   This is an accident of hourly proof,
   Which I mistrusted not: farewell therefore, Hero.

Enter BENEDICK

BENEDICK Count Claudio.
CLAUDIO Yea, the same.   140
BENEDICK Come, will you go with me?
CLAUDIO Whither?
BENEDICK Even to the next willow, about your own business, county:
  what fashion will you wear the garland of? About your neck, like an
  usurer's chain? Or under your arm, like a lieutenant's scarf? You 145
  must wear it one way, for the prince hath got your Hero.
CLAUDIO I wish him joy of her.
BENEDICK Why that's spoken like an honest drovier, so they sell bull-
  ocks: but did you think the prince would have served you thus?
CLAUDIO I pray you leave me.   150
BENEDICK Ho now you strike like the blind man, 'twas the boy that stole
  your meat, and you'll beat the post.
CLAUDIO If it will not be, I'll leave you.   *Exit*
BENEDICK Alas poor hurt fowl, now will he creep into sedges: but that my
  Lady Beatrice should know me, and not know me: the prince's fool! 155
  Hah, it may be I go under that title because I am merry: yea but so I
  am apt to do myself wrong: I am not so reputed, it is the base (though
  bitter) disposition of Beatrice, that puts the world into her person,
  and so gives me out: well, I'll be revenged as I may.

Benedick accuses Don Pedro of stealing Hero for himself. The prince declares
that he has kept his promise to Claudio. Benedick angrily relates how
Beatrice had insulted him during the dance.

1 How do you criticise a prince? (in pairs)

Imagine that you are at an office Christmas party and you see your
boss getting very familiar with the wife/husband of your best friend.
Improvise a conversation with your boss in which you try to express
your anger and disapproval without putting your job at risk.

Now read lines 160–78 where Benedick faces the similarly difficult
task of criticising Don Pedro. How well does Benedick manage it, and
how happy is he with the prince's explanation (lines 177–8)?

2 Express Benedick's anger and frustration
(in groups of about six)

We are close to the climax of the feud between Benedick and
Beatrice. He describes her in lines 190–7:

- Beatrice is Ate, the goddess of discord, who lived by the gates of
  hell. Benedick wants her 'conjured' back there. Men now
  deliberately sin to be sent to hell and out of Beatrice's way.

- Beatrice debilitates men, just as the Queen of Lydia enslaved the
  mighty Hercules (see page 182). In Beatrice's company Benedick
  feels like a man used as target practice ('at a mark') by an army of
  archers.

Read aloud lines 181–97, handing over to the next person at each
colon or full stop. Use a chair to represent Beatrice and direct your
anger and frustration towards it, using both voice and gesture.

List four phrases which create the best picture of this fearsome
woman and decide which of Beatrice's taunts has hurt Benedick most
of all.

Lady Fame Rumour
lodge . . . warren lonely hut in a
  hunting park
flat transgression simple offence
amiss in vain
my very visor even my mask

a great thaw slush and mud
impossible
  conveyance unbelievable trickery
poniards daggers
terminations way she uses words
turned spit turned the roasting spit

Enter DON PEDRO

DON PEDRO Now, signor, where's the count, did you see him?   160

BENEDICK Troth, my lord, I have played the part of Lady Fame, I found
    him here as melancholy as a lodge in a warren; I told him, and I think I
    told him true, that your grace had got the good will of this young lady,
    and I offered him my company to a willow tree, either to make him a
    garland, as being forsaken, or to bind him up a rod, as being worthy to   165
    be whipped.

DON PEDRO To be whipped: what's his fault?

BENEDICK The flat transgression of a schoolboy, who being overjoyed
    with finding a bird's nest, shows it his companion, and he steals it.

DON PEDRO Wilt thou make a trust a transgression? The transgression is   170
    in the stealer.

BENEDICK Yet it had not been amiss the rod had been made, and the
    garland too, for the garland he might have worn himself, and the rod
    he might have bestowed on you, who (as I take it) have stolen his
    bird's nest.   175

DON PEDRO I will but teach them to sing, and restore them to the owner.

BENEDICK If their singing answer your saying, by my faith, you say
    honestly.

DON PEDRO The Lady Beatrice hath a quarrel to you, the gentleman that
    danced with her told her she is much wronged by you.   180

BENEDICK Oh she misused me past the endurance of a block: an oak but
    with one green leaf on it, would have answered her: my very visor
    began to assume life, and scold with her: she told me, not thinking I
    had been myself, that I was the prince's jester, that I was duller than a
    great thaw, huddling jest upon jest, with such impossible conveyance   185
    upon me, that I stood like a man at a mark, with a whole army shooting
    at me: she speaks poniards, and every word stabs: if her breath were
    as terrible as her terminations, there were no living near her, she
    would infect to the north star: I would not marry her, though she were
    endowed with all that Adam had left him before he transgressed: she   190
    would have made Hercules have turned spit, yea, and have cleft his
    club to make the fire too: come, talk not of her, you shall find her the
    infernal Ate in good apparel. I would to God some scholar would
    conjure her, for certainly, while she is here, a man may live as quiet in
    hell, as in a sanctuary, and people sin upon purpose, because they   195
    would go thither, so indeed all disquiet, horror and perturbation
    follows her.

Benedick, in hugely extravagant fashion, leaves to avoid meeting Beatrice. She hints that they may have loved each other once. Don Pedro informs Claudio that he has won Hero's hand on Claudio's behalf.

1 Excuses (in groups of three)

Some productions have made this a comic yet painful moment with Beatrice overhearing much of what Benedick says in lines 193–208.

a 'I'd rather go to the ends of the earth.' In hyperbolic language (lines 199–205), Benedick volunteers to undertake the most fantastic tasks for Don Pedro to avoid speaking to Beatrice. Use hyperbole to invent a similar set of things that you would volunteeer to do to avoid an embarrassing or painful meeting.

b Try lines 193–217 in different ways . . . play it for comedy, or pain, or both. Talk together about what is going through the minds of Beatrice and Benedick.

2 How did the Beatrice–Benedick feud start? (in pairs)

Take a part each and read lines 209–16 aloud several times. Does Beatrice hint in any way at the reasons for her hostility towards Benedick?

3 Show Claudio's discomfort (in groups of five)

Don Pedro and Leonato keep Claudio in suspense for a moment before revealing their surprise.

- Rehearse the betrothal scene (lines 216–40). Show Claudio's unhappiness and the secret amusement of Don Pedro and Leonato. Is Hero also happy?

- 'Civil, count, civil as an orange.' Beatrice (lines 222–4) puns on 'civil' and 'Seville'. A Seville orange is bitter-tasting and yellowish in colour. How apt a description of Claudio is this pun?

Antipodes opposite side of the world
tooth-picker a maker of toothpicks
Prester John legendary Christian king in Africa or Asia

Great Cham emperor of the Mongols
embassage errand
Harpy fierce bird-like monster with a beautiful female face
blazon description
conceit belief

Enter CLAUDIO *and* BEATRICE, LEONATO [*and*] HERO

DON PEDRO Look, here she comes.

BENEDICK Will your grace command me any service to the world's end? I
will go on the slightest errand now to the Antipodes that you can   200
devise to send me on: I will fetch you a tooth-picker now from the
furthest inch of Asia: bring you the length of Prester John's foot: fetch
you a hair off the Great Cham's beard: do you any embassage to the
Pygmies, rather than hold three words conference with this Harpy:
you have no employment for me?   205

DON PEDRO None, but to desire your good company.

BENEDICK Oh God, sir, here's a dish I love not, I cannot endure my Lady
Tongue.   *Exit*

DON PEDRO Come, lady, come, you have lost the heart of Signor
Benedick.   210

BEATRICE Indeed, my lord, he lent it me a while, and I gave him use for it,
a double heart for his single one: marry once before he won it of me,
with false dice, therefore your grace may well say I have lost it.

DON PEDRO You have put him down, lady, you have put him down.

BEATRICE So I would not he should do me, my lord, lest I should prove   215
the mother of fools: I have brought Count Claudio, whom you sent
me to seek.

DON PEDRO Why how now, count, wherefore are you sad?

CLAUDIO Not sad, my lord.

DON PEDRO How then? Sick?   220

CLAUDIO Neither, my lord.

BEATRICE The count is neither sad, nor sick, nor merry, nor well: but
civil, count, civil as an orange, and something of that jealous
complexion.

DON PEDRO I'faith, lady, I think your blazon to be true, though I'll be   225
sworn, if he be so, his conceit is false: here, Claudio, I have wooed in
thy name, and fair Hero is won: I have broke with her father, and his
good will obtained: name the day of marriage, and God give thee joy.

Claudio and Hero are betrothed. Beatrice jokingly complains that she is now the only one left without a husband. Don Pedro offers himself as a candidate but Beatrice refuses.

1 Thoughts of a father (in groups of five)

From the moment when he betrothes his daughter to Claudio (lines 229–30) until he instructs his niece to run an errand for him (line 256), Leonato watches silently. But what might he be thinking? Take a part each and rehearse lines 229–57. Decide on the moves and reactions he might make.

Then devise a presentation where the characters 'freeze' every few lines to allow Leonato to say what he is thinking at that moment. Show your version to the rest of the class.

2 Thoughts of a prince (in pairs)

What exactly are Beatrice and Don Pedro up to in lines 241–55? Take parts, then stand or sit face to face and speak your lines in the following ways:

- as Beatrice flirts with Don Pedro he makes a light-hearted proposal which she gently turns down
- Don Pedro makes a serious proposal which Beatrice politely rejects
- Don Pedro makes a serious proposal which Beatrice bluntly, almost cruelly, turns down
- Beatrice's boldness in inviting a prince to propose to her offends Don Pedro and she quickly has to apologise.

Talk about the different pictures of Don Pedro that these versions create. Which portrait do you prefer?

---

all grace God
windy side away from (a sailing ship kept upwind to avoid attack)
alliance relatives (which of Claudio's words has surprised her?)
goes . . . world gets married

sunburnt unattractive
getting offspring ('fathering')
no matter never seriously
star . . . born i.e. the dancing star influenced her personality
cry . . . mercy forgive me

LEONATO Count, take of me my daughter, and with her my fortunes: his
　　grace hath made the match, and all grace say amen to it.　　　230
BEATRICE Speak, count, 'tis your cue.
CLAUDIO Silence is the perfectest herald of joy, I were but little happy if I
　　could say, how much! Lady, as you are mine, I am yours: I give away
　　myself for you, and dote upon the exchange.
BEATRICE Speak, cousin, or (if you cannot) stop his mouth with a kiss,　　235
　　and let not him speak neither.
DON PEDRO In faith, lady, you have a merry heart.
BEATRICE Yea, my lord, I thank it, poor fool it keeps on the windy side of
　　care: my cousin tells him in his ear that he is in her heart.
CLAUDIO And so she doth, cousin.　　　240
BEATRICE Good Lord for alliance: thus goes every one to the world but I,
　　and I am sunburnt, I may sit in a corner and cry, 'Heigh ho for a
　　husband.'
DON PEDRO Lady Beatrice, I will get you one.
BEATRICE I would rather have one of your father's getting: hath your　　245
　　grace ne'er a brother like you? Your father got excellent husbands, if a
　　maid could come by them.
DON PEDRO Will you have me, lady?
BEATRICE No, my lord, unless I might have another for working-days,
　　your grace is too costly to wear every day: but I beseech your grace　　250
　　pardon me, I was born to speak all mirth, and no matter.
DON PEDRO Your silence most offends me, and to be merry, best
　　becomes you, for out a question, you were born in a merry hour.
BEATRICE No sure, my lord, my mother cried, but then there was a star
　　danced, and under that was I born: cousins, God give you joy.　　255
LEONATO Niece, will you look to those things I told you of?
BEATRICE I cry you mercy, uncle: by your grace's pardon.　　　*Exit*

The marriage of Hero and Claudio is set for a week ahead.
Don Pedro proposes some entertainment for the interim. He will make
Beatrice and Benedick fall in love with each other.

---

1 'She were an excellent wife for Benedick'
(in small groups)

Look back over events so far and find as many serious reasons as you
can for agreeing with Don Pedro. Then give as many reasons as you
can for agreeing with Leonato when he says 'Oh Lord!'.

2 'There's little of the melancholy element in her'

Many Elizabethans still held to the old belief that there were four
humours (or fluids) in the human body. They gave rise to four basic
types of personality, depending on which humour was predominant:

Melancholy (cold and dry)   cold, gloomy, depressed (melancholic)
Choler (hot and dry)   angry, quarrelsome, violent (choleric)
Phlegm (cool and moist)   cool, sluggish, apathetic (phlegmatic)
Blood (warm and moist)   warm, hopeful, confident (sanguine).

Assign each character in the play their most appropriate 'humour'.
You may well have differences in opinion here. Shakespeare's
characters are rather more complex than the medieval system of
humours!

3 An overview of the whole scene (in groups of ten or more)

In the theatre this scene can be spectacular, full of colour, stage
'busyness', clever conversation, dancing and music. Devise your own
mini-version of this scene using no more than fifty words of the
original script. Include mime, gesture and movement to give it vitality.
You could also make masks and select suitable music.

---

out of suit out of pursuing her
rites (1) religious rites of marriage
  (2) rites as a husband
a just seven-night exactly a week
answer my mind arranged as I
  want them

Hercules' labours see page 182
fain gladly
honesty worth, honour
practise on deceive, work on
queasy stomach weak disposition
my drift what I propose

DON PEDRO By my troth a pleasant spirited lady.

LEONATO There's little of the melancholy element in her, my lord, she is never sad, but when she sleeps, and not ever sad then: for I have heard my daughter say, she hath often dreamed of unhappiness, and waked herself with laughing. 260

DON PEDRO She cannot endure to hear tell of a husband.

LEONATO Oh by no means, she mocks all her wooers out of suit.

DON PEDRO She were an excellent wife for Benedick. 265

LEONATO Oh Lord, my lord, if they were but a week married, they would talk themselves mad.

DON PEDRO County Claudio, when mean you to go to church?

CLAUDIO Tomorrow, my lord: time goes on crutches, till love have all his rites. 270

LEONATO Not till Monday, my dear son, which is hence a just seven-night, and a time too brief too, to have all things answer my mind.

DON PEDRO Come, you shake the head at so long a breathing, but I warrant thee, Claudio, the time shall not go dully by us. I will in the interim undertake one of Hercules' labours, which is, to bring Signor 275 Benedick and the Lady Beatrice into a mountain of affection, th'one with th'other: I would fain have it a match, and I doubt not but to fashion it, if you three will but minister such assistance as I shall give you direction.

LEONATO My lord, I am for you, though it cost me ten nights' watchings. 280

CLAUDIO And I, my lord.

DON PEDRO And you too, gentle Hero?

HERO I will do any modest office, my lord, to help my cousin to a good husband.

DON PEDRO And Benedick is not the unhopefullest husband that I know: 285 thus far can I praise him, he is of a noble strain, of approved valour, and confirmed honesty. I will teach you how to humour your cousin, that she shall fall in love with Benedick, and I, with your two helps, will so practise on Benedick, that in despite of his quick wit, and his queasy stomach, he shall fall in love with Beatrice: if we can do this, 290 Cupid is no longer an archer, his glory shall be ours, for we are the only love-gods. Go in with me, and I will tell you my drift.

Exeunt

Don John's first plot against Claudio has failed. Borachio now proposes a much more dishonest scheme which will trick Claudio and Don Pedro into believing that Hero is unfaithful.

1 The sky begins to darken (in small groups)

Beatrice and Benedick's friends are planning some innocent amusement at their expense. Don John and Borachio have a more unpleasant aim – to ruin Hero's honour.

a Evil and villainy

Two of you read this scene aloud. The rest repeat or echo all the 'evil' or 'villainous' words that are spoken. Decide which of the two men is the greater villain, and why.

b Images of disease and death

How many sickness/death words do Don John and Borachio use as they discuss their plan?

2 The villains intervene, but where and when?
(in groups of six)

Neither the time nor the setting for this scene were made clear in early editions of the play. It could be inside Leonato's house, in his garden, or outside in the street. Neither is it clear whether the action follows on immediately from the end of Scene 1, or whether some time has elapsed.

Take a part each and read the final lines of the previous scene (lines 287–92) together with the opening lines of this scene (lines 1–10). Decide where and when you think this new scene should be set. Give reasons to justify your decision.

---

comes . . . affection frustrates his desires
ranges . . . mine satisfies me
unseasonable inappropriate
temper mix, prepare

whose estimation . . . hold up whose honour you most strongly proclaim
contaminated stale diseased prostitute
misuse deceive
issue outcome

ACT 2   SCENE 2
Leonato's house

Enter DON JOHN and BORACHIO

DON JOHN It is so, the Count Claudio shall marry the daughter of
Leonato.

BORACHIO Yea, my lord, but I can cross it.

DON JOHN Any bar, any cross, any impediment, will be medicinable to
me, I am sick in displeasure to him, and whatsoever comes athwart his   5
affection, ranges evenly with mine. How canst thou cross this
marriage?

BORACHIO Not honestly, my lord, but so covertly, that no dishonesty
shall appear in me.

DON JOHN Show me briefly how.   10

BORACHIO I think I told your lordship a year since, how much I am in the
favour of Margaret, the waiting gentlewoman to Hero.

DON JOHN I remember.

BORACHIO I can at any unseasonable instant of the night, appoint her to
look out at her lady's chamber window.   15

DON JOHN What life is in that to be the death of this marriage?

BORACHIO The poison of that lies in you to temper; go you to the prince
your brother, spare not to tell him, that he hath wronged his honour in
marrying the renowned Claudio, whose estimation do you mightily
hold up, to a contaminated stale, such a one as Hero.   20

DON JOHN What proof shall I make of that?

BORACHIO Proof enough, to misuse the prince, to vex Claudio, to undo
Hero, and kill Leonato; look you for any other issue?

DON JOHN Only to despite them I will endeavour anything.

Borachio's plan is that he and Margaret will appear that night at Hero's bedroom window. They will call each other Hero and Claudio, so deceiving the watching Don Pedro and Claudio.

Borachio outlines his plan to Don John.

1 Honour, reputation and virginity

How many times are these three virtues mentioned in this scene? People have so far talked of such matters with casual and light-hearted confidence. Borachio's plan, with its talk of 'semblance' (outward show) and 'seeming truth', will test everyone's moral soundness.

meet suitable
intend pretend you have
zeal earnestness
as in love of as if you were concerned for
like to be about to be

cozened cheated
trial proof
jealousy . . . assurance mere suspicion will become certainty
ducats Italian silver coins

BORACHIO Go then, find me a meet hour to draw Don Pedro and the   25
Count Claudio alone, tell them that you know that Hero loves me,
intend a kind of zeal both to the prince and Claudio (as in love of your
brother's honour who hath made this match, and his friend's reputation, who is thus like to be cozened with the semblance of a maid)
that you have discovered thus: they will scarcely believe this without   30
trial: offer them instances which shall bear no less likelihood, than to
see me at her chamber window, hear me call Margaret Hero, hear
Margaret term me Claudio, and bring them to see this the very night
before the intended wedding, for in the mean time, I will so fashion
the matter, that Hero shall be absent, and there shall appear such   35
seeming truth of Hero's disloyalty, that jealousy shall be called
assurance, and all the preparation overthrown.

DON JOHN Grow this to what adverse issue it can, I will put it in practice:
be cunning in the working this, and thy fee is a thousand ducats.

BORACHIO Be you constant in the accusation, and my cunning shall not   40
shame me.

DON JOHN I will presently go learn their day of marriage.

Exeunt

Benedick muses on men like Claudio who say they will not fall in love and then do so. He lists the virtues required of his own future wife. Benedick hides when he sees the prince, Claudio, and Leonato approach.

1 When does the boy return?

The script does not tell us! Some productions have set up a running joke as the boy chases through scene after scene vainly attempting to deliver Benedick's book. After reading through this scene, decide where the boy might most amusingly attempt to give Benedick the book.

2 Claudio – before and after (in groups of three)

Benedick (lines 7–17) can scarcely believe the change in his friend's behaviour. One of you takes the role of Claudio as he used to be, another plays him as he is now. The third person is Benedick who introduces the two Claudios to the class and tells the whole sorry story. Use your own words and/or words from the script.

3 Benedick's ideal woman (in groups of six)

In lines 18–27 Benedick lists the feminine virtues he is immune to, then lists the qualities that might tempt him if they were all to be found in one woman.

Write a list of the qualities you seek in your ideal partner. Then incorporate your list into a speech which uses word patterns similar to Benedick's (for example, 'another is ... yet I am well', 'wise or I'll ...').

Present your speech to the class using all the members of the group.

---

am ... already will do it at once (Benedick takes him literally)
argument object
drum ... fife music of war
tabor ... pipe music of peace
carving designing

turned orthography speaks an elaborate, flowery language
oyster i.e. shut up in moody silence
well not ill with love
cheapen make an offer for
noble/angel names of coins

ACT 2   SCENE 3
Leonato's orchard

Enter BENEDICK *alone*

BENEDICK Boy.
BOY [*within*] Signor.

[*Enter* BOY]

BENEDICK In my chamber window lies a book, bring it hither to me in
  the orchard.
BOY I am here already, sir.   5
BENEDICK I know that, but I would have thee hence and here again.
Exit [*Boy*]

I do much wonder, that one man seeing how much another man is a
fool, when he dedicates his behaviours to love, will after he hath
laughed at such shallow follies in others, become the argument of
his own scorn, by falling in love: and such a man is Claudio. I have   10
known when there was no music with him but the drum and the fife,
and now had he rather hear the tabor and the pipe: I have known
when he would have walked ten mile afoot, to see a good armour,
and now will he lie ten nights awake carving the fashion of a new
doublet: he was wont to speak plain and to the purpose (like an   15
honest man and a soldier) and now is he turned orthography, his
words are a very fantastical banquet, just so many strange dishes:
may I be so converted and see with these eyes? I cannot tell, I think
not: I will not be sworn but love may transform me to an oyster, but
I'll take my oath on it, till he have made an oyster of me, he shall   20
never make me such a fool/one woman is fair, yet I am well: another
is wise, yet I am well: another virtuous, yet I am well: but till all
graces be in one woman, one woman shall not come in my grace:
rich she shall be, that's certain: wise, or I'll none: virtuous, or I'll
never cheapen her: fair, or I'll never look on her: mild, or come not   25
near me: noble, or not I for an angel: of good discourse, an excellent
musician – and her hair shall be of what colour it please God. Hah!
the prince and Monsieur Love, I will hide me in the arbour.

*Don Pedro, Claudio and Leonato pretend not to notice the hidden Benedick.
They prepare to listen to Balthasar's singing. Benedick is not impressed
by the romantic music.*

1 Where does Benedick hide? (in small groups)

Look at the picture on page 54 to see an example of where one
Benedick hid himself. This Benedick loved to smoke cigars, so puffs
of smoke rose from inside the tree as he listened to his friends'
conversation.

Imagine that you are staging a production of *Much Ado About
Nothing* at your school or college. Talk about where you would hide
Benedick. It would need to be where he could be heard as well as
seen by the audience. Is there anywhere in your school or college
grounds that is suitable for an open-air production of the play? If so,
where would Benedick hide?

2 Poetry and prose (in small groups)

This is the third occasion in the play where characters speak in blank
verse (lines 30–48). Choose a few lines or phrases from this section
that you like. Read them aloud to each other and talk about the mood
these verse lines create for you.

The unromantic Benedick interrupts in prose when he realises that
Balthasar is about to sing a love song. One of you reads lines 50–2.
Which man does Benedick's comment refer to? What different mood,
or tone is created by these prose lines?

3 Nothing and noting again (in pairs)

Take a part each and read aloud lines 44–9. Practise saying these
lines in a way that highlights the word-play on 'notes', 'noting',
'nothing'. Compare this exchange with 1.1.119–20. What extra
meaning does Balthasar give to the word 'note'?

---

fit . . . pennyworth give Benedick
  more than he bargains for
tax not do not order
slander bring disgrace on
witness still always a sign
put . . . face on pretend not to
  recognise

do it in notes be brief
crotchets (1) fanciful ideas (2)
  notes in music
sheep's guts strings of a lute
hale draw, fetch

Enter DON PEDRO, LEONATO, CLAUDIO *and* BALTHASAR *with music*

DON PEDRO Come, shall we hear this music?
CLAUDIO Yea, my good lord: how still the evening is,   30
    As hushed on purpose to grace harmony!
DON PEDRO See you where Benedick hath hid himself?
CLAUDIO Oh very well, my lord: the music ended,
    We'll fit the kid-fox with a pennyworth.
DON PEDRO Come, Balthasar, we'll hear that song again.   35
BALTHASAR Oh, good my lord, tax not so bad a voice,
    To slander music any more than once.
DON PEDRO It is the witness still of excellency,
    To put a strange face on his own perfection:
    I pray thee sing, and let me woo no more.   40
BALTHASAR Because you talk of wooing I will sing,
    Since many a wooer doth commence his suit,
    To her he thinks not worthy, yet he woos,
    Yet will he swear he loves.
DON PEDRO   Nay, pray thee come,
    Or if thou wilt hold longer argument,   45
    Do it in notes.
BALTHASAR   Note this before my notes,
    There's not a note of mine that's worth the noting.
DON PEDRO Why these are very crotchets that he speaks,
    Note notes forsooth, and nothing.
               [Music]
BENEDICK Now divine air, now is his soul ravished: is it not strange that   50
  sheep's guts should hale souls out of men's bodies? Well, a horn for
  my money when all's done.

Balthasar sings his song about the fickleness of men. He is sent by Don Pedro to prepare the music that will be used to serenade Hero at her chamber window the next night.

1 'Men were deceivers ever . . .' (in pairs)

Balthasar's song comes at a turning point in the play and sounds a mocking echo to one of the central preoccupations of the play . . . deception.

- Read alternate lines of the song to your partner and talk about why Benedick and Claudio may soon discover that the words of the song apply to them.
- Think of the many examples of deception practised so far in the play. Have they have all been perpetrated by men?

2 Is the song sung well?

How impressed are Don Pedro and Benedick with Balthasar's singing (lines 69–75)? If you were producing the play, would you have the song sung well or badly? Talk about:

- the effect of a movingly beautiful song heard at this moment
- the effect that bad singing would create.

You could also try setting the song to appropriate music.

3 Why is this interlude here?

Why don't we go straight on with the tricking of Benedick? Think of at least four reasons why Shakespeare included lines 29–80.

---

blithe and bonny cheerful and carefree
no mo no more
dumps sad songs
fraud faithlessness
leavy full of leaves, ' leaf-y'

for a shift for want of someone better
And he if he
as lief rather
night-raven its harsh cry foretold death or sickness

The Song

[BALTHASAR] Sigh no more, ladies, sigh no more,
   Men were deceivers ever,
  One foot in sea, and one on shore,   55
   To one thing constant never.
  Then sigh not so, but let them go,
   And be you blithe and bonny,
  Converting all your sounds of woe,
   Into hey nonny nonny.   60

  Sing no more ditties, sing no mo,
   Of dumps so dull and heavy,
  The fraud of men was ever so,
   Since summer first was leavy.
  Then sigh not so, but let them go,   65
   And be you blithe and bonny,
  Converting all your sounds of woe,
   Into hey nonny nonny.

DON PEDRO By my troth a good song.

BALTHASAR And an ill singer, my lord.   70

DON PEDRO Ha, no no faith, thou sing'st well enough for a shift.

BENEDICK And he had been a dog that should have howled thus, they
  would have hanged him: and I pray God his bad voice bode no
  mischief, I had as lief have heard the night-raven, come what plague
  could have come after it.   75

DON PEDRO Yea marry, dost thou hear, Balthasar? I pray thee get us
  some excellent music: for tomorrow night we would have it at the
  Lady Hero's chamber window.

BALTHASAR The best I can, my lord.

DON PEDRO Do so, farewell.   80

           Exit Balthasar

Don Pedro and the others begin their deception of Benedick. They talk about how Beatrice is madly in love with Benedick, but dares not tell him of her love.

1 The fooling of Benedick (in groups of five)

The trick ('gull') Benedick's friends play on him makes marvellous theatre. To get a first impression, and to see if their plot works, read through lines 81–213. Then explore Benedick's reactions.

The 1990 Royal Shakespeare Company production had Benedick hiding in a tree and peering through the foliage. He puffed smoke from his cigar, coughed, choked, and at one point fell out of the tree.

Prepare your version of lines 81–180. Show the enjoyment of Benedick's friends as they set about their plan. Which lines do the plotters whisper to themselves and which do they say deliberately loudly for Benedick's benefit?

Work out how to 'hide' Benedick so that your audience can still see his reactions (surprise, anger, pleasure, curiosity, hurt?).

Show your version to the rest of the class.

---

stalk on . . . sits start your hunting, the game bird has settled

Sits . . . corner? is that really the way things are?

it . . . thought it is unbelievable, but true

counterfeit pretend

near . . . passion close to real passion

discovers it shows it

hold it up keep it going

smock slip, undergarment

Come hither, Leonato, what was it you told me of today, that your
niece Beatrice was in love with Signor Benedick?

CLAUDIO Oh aye, stalk on, stalk on, the fowl sits. I did never think that
lady would have loved any man.

LEONATO No nor I neither, but most wonderful, that she should so dote   85
on Signor Benedick, whom she hath in all outward behaviours
seemed ever to abhor.

BENEDICK Is't possible? Sits the wind in that corner?

LEONATO By my troth, my lord, I cannot tell what to think of it, but that
she loves him with an enraged affection, it is past the infinite of   90
thought.

DON PEDRO May be she doth but counterfeit.

CLAUDIO Faith like enough.

LEONATO Oh God! Counterfeit? There was never counterfeit of passion, came so near the life of passion as she discovers it.   95

DON PEDRO Why what effects of passion shows she?

CLAUDIO Bait the hook well, this fish will bite.

LEONATO What effects, my lord? She will sit you – you heard my
daughter tell you how.

CLAUDIO She did indeed.   100

DON PEDRO How, how, I pray you! You amaze me, I would have
thought her spirit had been invincible against all assaults of
affection.

LEONATO I would have sworn it had, my lord, especially against
Benedick.   105

BENEDICK I should think this a gull, but that the white-bearded fellow
speaks it: knavery cannot sure hide himself in such reverence.

CLAUDIO He hath ta'en th'infection, hold it up.

DON PEDRO Hath she made her affection known to Benedick?

LEONATO No, and swears she never will, that's her torment.   110

CLAUDIO 'Tis true indeed, so your daughter says: shall I, says she, that
have so oft encountered him with scorn, write to him that I love
him?

LEONATO This says she now when she is beginning to write to him, for
she'll be up twenty times a night, and there will she sit in her smock,   115
till she have writ a sheet of paper: my daughter tells us all.

Don Pedro and the others talk about Beatrice's many fine qualities.
They express their fear that Benedick will mock her if he learns of her great
love for him.

1 Give it all you've got! (in groups of four)

The plan is going well and Benedick's three friends are enjoying themselves.

Take a part each (the fourth person is the listening Benedick) and read lines 122–59 at least twice. Express your concern for Beatrice and angry outrage at Benedick and his faults. Ask Benedick which comments about him hit home the hardest.

In the very first scene, Benedick admitted that Beatrice would be a beautiful woman if only 'she were not possessed with a fury' (1.1.141). How do the three men convince Benedick that Beatrice is madly in love with him, and how do they persuade him to fall in love with her (lines 85–154)?

2 'I would she had bestowed this dotage on me'

Don Pedro has already asked Beatrice to marry him (2.1.241–57). Do you think he was serious then? Is he serious in lines 144–5 when he says that he wishes Beatrice were in love with him? If the prince were played as genuinely being in love with Beatrice, how would that affect your perception of his character and hers?

3 Beatrice the orphan

One famous actress who played Beatrice said that she saw the character as 'a poor family relation living off her wits'. Find the line which suggests that Beatrice has no parents. Does this fact help to explain why Leonato and Antonio treat Beatrice so differently to Hero?

---

sheet (1) paper (2) bed linen
flout mock, ridicule
ecstasy frenzy, passion
by some other from someone else
discover it reveal it
And he should if he did

alms a good deed
blood passion
daffed . . . respects put aside all other considerations
bate give up, abate
tender an offer

CLAUDIO Now you talk of a sheet of paper, I remember a pretty jest your daughter told us of.

LEONATO Oh when she had writ it, and was reading it over, she found Benedick and Beatrice between the sheet. 120

CLAUDIO That.

LEONATO Oh she tore the letter into a thousand halfpence, railed at herself, that she should be so immodest to write to one that she knew would flout her: I measure him, says she, by my own spirit, for I should flout him, if he writ to me, yea, though I love him I should. 125

CLAUDIO Then down upon her knees she falls, weeps, sobs, beats her heart, tears her hair, prays, curses, Oh sweet Benedick, God give me patience.

LEONATO She doth indeed, my daughter says so, and the ecstasy hath so much overborn her, that my daughter is sometime afeared she 130 will do a desperate outrage to herself, it is very true.

DON PEDRO It were good that Benedick knew of it by some other, if she will not discover it.

CLAUDIO To what end? He would make but a sport of it, and torment the poor lady worse. 135

DON PEDRO And he should, it were an alms to hang him: she's an excellent sweet lady, and (out of all suspicion) she is virtuous.

CLAUDIO And she is exceeding wise.

DON PEDRO In everything but in loving Benedick.

LEONATO Oh my lord, wisdom and blood combating in so tender a 140 body, we have ten proofs to one, that blood hath the victory: I am sorry for her, as I have just cause, being her uncle, and her guardian.

DON PEDRO I would she had bestowed this dotage on me, I would have daffed all other respects, and made her half myself: I pray you tell 145 Benedick of it, and hear what a will say.

LEONATO Were it good, think you?

CLAUDIO Hero thinks surely she will die, for she says she will die, if he love her not, and she will die ere she make her love known, and she will die if he woo her, rather than she will bate one breath of her 150 accustomed crossness.

DON PEDRO She doth well: if she should make tender of her love, 'tis very possible he'll scorn it, for the man (as you know all) hath a contemptible spirit.

Don Pedro, Claudio and Leonato leave, hoping they have completed their deception of Benedick. Don Pedro orders a similar trick to be played on Beatrice by Hero and her attendant gentlewomen.

1 Does Don Pedro go over the top?

List the compliments that Claudio and Leonato pay Benedick (lines 155–67). Notice how Don Pedro turns each compliment into a criticism. Do you think there is a point where the prince goes too far in his abuse of Benedick and almost gives the game away?

2 Why does Benedick believe them? (in pairs)

This is how one actor showed Benedick's reaction to what he overheard. He is amazed, but persuaded!

Before turning over to read what Benedick says, think of four reasons he might have for believing what his friends have 'revealed'.

proper handsome	**howsoever** even though
outward happiness pleasing outward appearance	**by . . . jests . . . make** judging by some of the rude jokes he tells
wit intelligence	**wear . . . counsel** bear it with good sense
Hector Trojan warrior hero	
a must he must	**dotage** passion

CLAUDIO He is a very proper man.   155

DON PEDRO He hath indeed a good outward happiness.

CLAUDIO Before God, and in my mind, very wise.

DON PEDRO He doth indeed show some sparks that are like wit.

LEONATO And I take him to be valiant.

DON PEDRO As Hector, I assure you, and in the managing of quarrels   160
you may say he is wise, for either he avoids them with great discre-
tion, or undertakes them with a most christianlike fear.

LEONATO If he do fear God, a must necessarily keep peace: if he break
the peace, he ought to enter into a quarrel with fear and trembling.

DON PEDRO And so will he do, for the man doth fear God, howsoever it   165
seems not in him, by some large jests he will make: well, I am sorry
for your niece: shall we go seek Benedick, and tell him of her love?

CLAUDIO Never tell him, my lord, let her wear it out with good counsel.

LEONATO Nay that's impossible, she may wear her heart out first.

DON PEDRO Well, we will hear further of it by your daughter, let it cool   170
the while: I love Benedick well, and I could wish he would modestly
examine himself, to see how much he is unworthy so good a lady.

LEONATO My lord, will you walk? Dinner is ready.

CLAUDIO If he do not dote on her upon this, I will never trust my
expectation.   175

DON PEDRO Let there be the same net spread for her, and that must
your daughter and her gentlewomen carry: the sport will be, when
they hold one an opinion of another's dotage, and no such matter:
that's the scene that I would see, which will be merely a dumb show:
let us send her to call him in to dinner.   180

                                        [*Exeunt all but Benedick*]

59

Benedick is convinced that Beatrice loves him and resolves to return her affection. When she appears to call him to dinner, he looks for signs of love in her.

1 'This can be no trick' (in pairs)

When leading a drama masterclass, the actress Janet Suzman argued that Benedick's opening words ('This can be no trick') have a tremendous impact. Experiment with saying this short phrase to each other in different ways (decisively, solemnly, excitedly and so on). Does the sequence of five monosyllabic words influence the way in which you say this line?

Now read Benedick's monologue (lines 181–200), taking a sentence each. Which of his remarks do you think the audience will find the funniest?

2 The new Benedick meets the old Beatrice
(in groups of four)

The last time they met, Benedick called Beatrice a Harpy. You can imagine the mood she is in when she is sent to collect him. But Benedick is a changed man! He has so far steadfastly refused to have anything to do with love, and has spoken nothing but prose. Find the line where, for a moment, he seems to speak to Beatrice in blank verse. What do you think Beatrice makes of it?

Two of you memorise lines 198–207 (from 'here comes Beatrice . . .'). The other two become Beatrice and Benedick's *alter egos* who must speak their character's inner thoughts as the conversation proceeds.

Prepare a script which combines these public words and unspoken thoughts. You could perhaps have the *alter egos* speaking from behind or beside each character. Rehearse your version and show it to the rest of the class.

---

the conference . . . sadly
  borne the conversation was a serious one
have . . . bent are stretched to their limit (like a bow)
censured judged
reprove deny
meat food

sentences witty sayings
awe frighten
career course
humour inclination
daw withal jackdaw with it
stomach appetite (for a fight)
Jew an object of abuse

BENEDICK This can be no trick, the conference was sadly borne, they
have the truth of this from Hero, they seem to pity the lady: it seems
her affections have their full bent: love me? Why, it must be
requited: I hear how I am censured, they say I will bear myself
proudly, if I perceive the love come from her: they say too, that she   185
will rather die than give any sign of affection: I did never think to
marry, I must not seem proud, happy are they that hear their detrac-
tions, and can put them to mending: they say the lady is fair, 'tis a
truth, I can bear them witness: and virtuous, 'tis so, I cannot reprove
it: and wise, but for loving me: by my troth it is no addition to her   190
wit, nor no great argument of her folly, for I will be horribly in love
with her: I may chance have some odd quirks and remnants of wit
broken on me, because I have railed so long against marriage: but
doth not the appetite alter? A man loves the meat in his youth, that
he cannot endure in his age. Shall quips and sentences, and these   195
paper bullets of the brain awe a man from the career of his humour?
No, the world must be peopled. When I said I would die a bachelor,
I did not think I should live till I were married – here comes
Beatrice: by this day, she's a fair lady, I do spy some marks of love in
her.   200

Enter BEATRICE

BEATRICE Against my will I am sent to bid you come in to dinner.
BENEDICK Fair Beatrice, I thank you for your pains.
BEATRICE I took no more pains for those thanks, than you took pains to
thank me, if it had been painful I would not have come.
BENEDICK You take pleasure then in the message.   205
BEATRICE Yea, just so much as you may take upon a knife's point, and
choke a daw withal: you have no stomach, signor, fare you well. *Exit*
BENEDICK Ha, against my will I am sent to bid you come in to dinner:
there's a double meaning in that: I took no more pains for those
thanks than you take pains to thank me: that's as much as to say, any   210
pains that I take for you is as easy as thanks: if I do not take pity of
her I am a villain, if I do not love her I am a Jew, I will go get her
picture.   *Exit*

Looking back at Act 2

1 Favourite lines

Look back through Act 2 and choose three or four lines that appeal to you. Make up a group and share your lines. Then present your version of the events in this act to the rest of the class using some or all of your favourite lines.

2 More masking and unmasking

Look back at the dance (2.1.61–114). Improvise what might have happened had this not been a masked dance. Which characters would have behaved differently and why?

3 Victorious or heart-broken?

Beatrice seems victorious in the battle of wits (2.1.103–7) when she calls Benedick 'the prince's jester'. She may feel less happy when Benedick later retaliates, branding her a 'Harpy' (2.1.201–5).

In pairs, devise two tableaux ('frozen moments') which show the feelings of Beatrice and Benedick at these two points in the play.

Show your two tableaux to the rest of the group. Hold each freeze for about thirty seconds so the group can study your expressions and gestures. After each tableau is shown, question Beatrice and Benedick, who must answer in role. Who is hurt more?

4 The joke show

Find as many different kinds of verbal and visual humour as you can in Act 2. Then devise a group presentation of these comic moments. At the end, ask your audience to identify the different sorts of humour in your sketches.

5 Patternings

Two pairs of lovers, two pairs of brothers, two conventional lovers, two unconventional lovers, two malevolent plots . . . and more!

Oppositions and patterns in the play are now becoming clearer. Write down as many pairings as you can. Who belongs in which pair?

Remember that the same character can appear in more than one pairing. For example, Claudio can be paired both as a friend and as a lover.

6 Sets and moods

There are many changes of mood and action in Act 2. What sites in and around your school or college would be most suitable for staging this act? Present your suggestions to the class, and be prepared to justify your choice.

7 Slapstick trickery

Choose your favourite moments and lines from the tricking of Benedick (Act 2 Scene 3). Using these lines, make up a high speed two-minute version which highlights Benedick's change from avowed bachelor to a man 'horribly in love'.

8 Balthasar's next song

After tricking Benedick, the friends go to Balthasar and ask him to write a comic song about deception and sighing lovers which they can sing to Benedick when next they meet. Write the song.

9 Men's talk

Write an extra scene for the play in which Don Pedro, Claudio, and Leonato talk about their deception of Benedick. Can you write it in a style of prose similar to that used in Act 2 Scene 3?

10 'Much ado about nothing' – double or triple meaning?

The play's title has at least two meanings, 'nothing' and 'noting' (see pages 10 and 50). Some people detect a third meaning: 'Much ado about virginity', because 'thing' in Elizabethan slang meant the female genitalia (nothing = no-thing). Do you think Act 2 can be used to justify this interpretation?

Hero begins her plan to trick Beatrice. Margaret is sent to tell Beatrice that Hero and Ursula are in the orchard talking about her. Beatrice steals in to eavesdrop on their conversation.

1 Find out how Beatrice is deceived (in pairs)

As Hero and Ursula, quickly read through the whole scene (ignore Margaret's one line) and see if the trick is played on Beatrice as you imagined it would be. Compare the women's tactics to those used by the men in the previous scene.

2 Show Hero's plan (in groups of three)

Take it in turns to be Hero. The space around you is the orchard. In the distance is the house where Beatrice and the men are. As Hero slowly reads lines 1–25, she must point clearly to every place and person mentioned. For example:

'Good Margaret (*point to Margaret*), run thee (*point again to Margaret*) to the parlour (*point to door*),
There shalt thou (*point to Margaret*) find my (*point to self*) cousin Beatrice . . .'

Lines 15–23 should not be read too quickly, otherwise Beatrice's entrance will appear too swift. Bearing this in mind, how would you stage these lines?

3 Sunshine and honeysuckle – princes and favourites

Lines 7–11 convey an impression of sunshine to match the orchard setting. The women are in a 'pleachèd bower', a shelter of intertwining branches, shaded from the sun by thickly growing honeysuckle.

Hero compares the honeysuckle to favoured noblemen who grow too proud and threaten to overwhelm their prince. How relevant do you think this simile is to the play? Decide which character it describes most accurately.

proposing talking
Ursley Ursula
favourites favoured courtiers

that power i.e. the power of the princes
propose conversation
crafty skilfully made, or cunning

ACT 3   SCENE 1
The orchard

Enter HERO *and two gentlewomen,* MARGARET *and* URSULA

HERO Good Margaret, run thee to the parlour,
　　　　There shalt thou find my cousin Beatrice,
　　　　Proposing with the prince and Claudio,
　　　　Whisper her ear and tell her I and Ursley
　　　　Walk in the orchard, and our whole discourse　　　　5
　　　　Is all of her, say that thou overheard'st us,
　　　　And bid her steal into the pleachèd bower,
　　　　Where honeysuckles ripened by the sun,
　　　　Forbid the sun to enter: like favourites,
　　　　Made proud by princes, that advance their pride,　　10
　　　　Against that power that bred it: there will she hide her,
　　　　To listen our propose: this is thy office,
　　　　Bear thee well in it, and leave us alone.
MARGARET I'll make her come I warrant you, presently.　　*Exit*
HERO Now, Ursula, when Beatrice doth come,　　　　15
　　　　As we do trace this alley up and down,
　　　　Our talk must only be of Benedick:
　　　　When I do name him, let it be thy part,
　　　　To praise him more than ever man did merit:
　　　　My talk to thee must be how Benedick　　　　20
　　　　Is sick in love with Beatrice: of this matter
　　　　Is little Cupid's crafty arrow made,
　　　　That only wounds by hearsay: now begin,

Enter BEATRICE

　　　　For look where Beatrice like a lapwing runs
　　　　Close by the ground, to hear our conference.　　25

Beatrice, thinking herself unobserved, listens in on Hero and Ursula's conversation. They begin to talk about Benedick's 'love' for Beatrice, and of her proud and scornful nature.

1 How would you stage the deception? (in groups of three)

There are many possible ways. Productions often dispense with the 'woodbine coverture' (shelter formed by the honeysuckle). One Beatrice, who hid herself in a swimming pool by the side of the stage, was forced at one point to submerge herself completely to avoid discovery. Another production 'hid' Beatrice in full view of the audience who saw every painful response to her friends' criticisms.

Present your version of lines 23–58 to the rest of the class. Stage it so that Beatrice's face and reactions can be seen by the audience.

2 Images of Beatrice (in small groups)

In lines 35–6 Hero says that Beatrice's spirits are 'as coy (disdainful) and wild as haggards of the rock'. A 'haggard' is a wild female hawk, which is far more difficult to train than one reared in captivity. How does this comparison help you to understand Beatrice's behaviour so far?

In lines 24–5 Hero compares Beatrice to a lapwing, a bird which searches for food by running along close to the ground, stopping and leaning forward to look for insects, before running on again. What does this suggest about the way Beatrice reaches her hiding place?

Find another 'creature image' used to describe Beatrice in lines 1–36. Does this comparison suggest that she will be easy or difficult to trick?

---

couchèd hidden
trothèd engaged, betrothed
wish . . . wrestle with get him to
 fight against
couch lie

Misprising despising
wit intelligence
take . . . affection take on any
 appearance or notion of love
self-endeared full of herself

URSULA   The pleasant'st angling is to see the fish
        Cut with her golden oars the silver stream,
        And greedily devour the treacherous bait:
        So angle we for Beatrice, who even now,
        Is couchèd in the woodbine coverture: 30
        Fear you not my part of the dialogue.
HERO   Then go we near her, that her ear lose nothing
        Of the false sweet bait that we lay for it:
        No truly, Ursula, she is too disdainful,
        I know her spirits are as coy and wild,   35
        As haggards of the rock.
URSULA   But are you sure,
        That Benedick loves Beatrice so entirely?
HERO   So says the prince, and my new trothèd lord.
URSULA   And did they bid you tell her of it, madam?
HERO   They did entreat me to acquaint her of it,   40
        But I persuaded them, if they loved Benedick,
        To wish him wrestle with affection,
        And never to let Beatrice know of it.
URSULA   Why did you so? Doth not the gentleman
        Deserve as full as fortunate a bed,   45
        As ever Beatrice shall couch upon?
HERO   Oh God of love! I know he doth deserve,
        As much as may be yielded to a man:
        But nature never framed a woman's heart
        Of prouder stuff than that of Beatrice: 50
        Disdain and scorn ride sparkling in her eyes,
        Misprising what they look on, and her wit
        Values itself so highly, that to her
        All matter else seems weak: she cannot love,
        Nor take no shape nor project of affection,   55
        She is so self-endeared.
URSULA   Sure I think so,
        And therefore certainly it were not good,
        She knew his love, lest she'll make sport at it.

Hero and Ursula talk about how Beatrice will never admit the true worth of any man, and how she would mock Benedick unmercifully if she knew he loved her. They then discuss Benedick's virtues.

1 Show Beatrice's opinion of men (in groups of about six)

In lines 61–70, Hero says that Beatrice loves to 'spell backward' every man she meets (i.e. to turn their virtues into faults).

Choose one man each from: the fair-faced, the black (dark-complexioned), the tall, the low (short), the speaking, the silent.

Each of you draw a cartoon picture of your man as Beatrice describes him. Show your group's collection to another group and ask them to match each picture to its appropriate description in the script.

2 Is Beatrice really like this? (in pairs)

Make a list of all the faults that Hero and Ursula find with Beatrice in lines 34–91. Match each of these character-flaws with a similar criticism made about Beatrice earlier in the play.

Do you think there is any truth in these remarks, or might Hero and Ursula be using this opportunity to get their own back on Beatrice?

3 'How much an ill word may empoison liking'

Lines 84–6 are an ominous reminder of an earlier conversation between Don John and Borachio in Act 2 Scene 2. Find the poison image in that scene which Hero's words unwittingly echo here.

---

antic grotesque figure
lance ill-headed badly-tipped
  spear
agate semi-precious stone
vilely cut crudely carved
vane weather vane

gives allows
simpleness simple honesty
purchaseth deserve
from all fashions out of step with
  everyone
honest innocent

HERO Why you speak truth, I never yet saw man,
   How wise, how noble, young, how rarely featured,   60
   But she would spell him backward: if fair-faced,
   She would swear the gentleman should be her sister:
   If black, why Nature drawing of an antic,
   Made a foul blot: if tall, a lance ill-headed:
   If low, an agate very vilely cut: 65
   If speaking, why a vane blown with all winds:
   If silent, why a block moved with none:
   So turns she every man the wrong side out,
   And never gives to truth and virtue, that
   Which simpleness and merit purchaseth.   70
URSULA Sure, sure, such carping is not commendable.
HERO No, not to be so odd, and from all fashions,
   As Beatrice is, cannot be commendable:
   But who dare tell her so? If I should speak,
   She would mock me into air, oh she would laugh me   75
   Out of myself, press me to death with wit:
   Therefore let Benedick like covered fire,
   Consume away in sighs, waste inwardly:
   It were a better death, than die with mocks,
   Which is as bad as die with tickling.   80
URSULA Yet tell her of it, hear what she will say.
HERO No rather I will go to Benedick,
   And counsel him to fight against his passion,
   And truly I'll devise some honest slanders,
   To stain my cousin with, one doth not know   85
   How much an ill word may empoison liking.
URSULA Oh do not do your cousin such a wrong,
   She cannot be so much without true judgement,
   Having so swift and excellent a wit,
   As she is prized to have, as to refuse   90
   So rare a gentleman as Signor Benedick.
HERO He is the only man of Italy,
   Always excepted my dear Claudio.

After more praise of Benedick, Hero and Ursula go inside to choose Hero's head-dress for tomorrow's wedding. Beatrice is amazed by what she has heard and resolves to return Benedick's love.

1 A new Beatrice (in groups of three)

Take it in turns to speak and act Beatrice's soliloquy (lines 107–16). Then try the following activities:

a Is Beatrice upset more by her gossiping friends or by the actual accusations? What change is there in her manner and opinions?

b This is the first time that Beatrice speaks in verse. Work out the **quatrain** and **couplet** rhyme patterns in what she says (a quatrain is a four-line rhyme pattern, a couplet is a two-line rhyme pattern). Remember that 'I' and '-ly' rhymed in Elizabethan times.

c Do her words resemble an Elizabethan love sonnet in any way (see page 177)?

2 Hero's parting couplet (in small groups)

Hero signals her exit with a rhyming couplet (lines 105–6) in which she voices one of the popular sayings of the time. Talk about the way the two pairs of lovers have fallen in love, then decide how much truth there is in what she says. Is falling in love mere chance, or the result of some mysterious power (like the influence of Cupid, the god of love)?

3 Review the scene (in groups of four)

Either: present a silent movie version of this scene
   or: improvise a modern scene where a friend is similarly tricked.

Speaking my fancy saying what I think
argument intelligent speech
tomorrow from tomorrow onwards
attires head-dresses or clothes
limed caught, trapped
by haps by chance

lives . . . such is gained by following such paths (of contempt and maiden pride)
band bond (of marriage)
reportingly just knowing it by what I have heard

URSULA I pray you be not angry with me, madam,
          Speaking my fancy: Signor Benedick,   95
          For shape, for bearing, argument and valour,
          Goes foremost in report through Italy.
HERO Indeed he hath an excellent good name.
URSULA His excellence did earn it, ere he had it:
          When are you married, madam?   100
HERO Why every day tomorrow: come go in,
          I'll show thee some attires, and have thy counsel,
          Which is the best to furnish me tomorrow.
URSULA She's limed I warrant you, we have caught her, madam.
HERO If it prove so, then loving goes by haps,   105
          Some Cupid kills with arrows, some with traps.
                                              Exeunt Hero and Ursula
BEATRICE What fire is in mine ears? Can this be true?
          Stand I condemned for pride and scorn so much?
          Contempt, farewell, and maiden pride, adieu,
          No glory lives behind the back of such.   110
          And Benedick, love on, I will requite thee,
          Taming my wild heart to thy loving hand:
          If thou dost love, my kindness shall incite thee
          To bind our loves up in a holy band,
          For others say thou dost deserve, and I   115
          Believe it better than reportingly.   *Exit*

Don Pedro plans to return to Arragon as soon as Claudio and Hero are married. The prince, Claudio and Leonato feign amazement at Benedick's lovelorn appearance and behaviour.

1 'Gallants, I am not as I have been' (in groups of four)

Benedick before.
Benedick after.

The new Benedick is quite a sight.

This is how one artist pictures Benedick's changed appearance. Talk about the 'before' and 'after' costumes you would choose for him.

Don Pedro talks of Benedick's immunity to the moodiness of love (lines 5–10), knowing full well that a silent, miserable Benedick stands beside him! Take a part each and tease Benedick (lines 1–54).

'Draw it! Hang it!'. 'Hang' could mean curse or execute. 'Draw' could mean pull out or disembowel prior to hanging someone. How do Don Pedro and Claudio play on these words to irritate Benedick?

---

consummate completed
vouchsafe me allow me
soil stain
hangman rascal
humour . . . worm Elizabethans believed both collected in hollow teeth causing toothache

grief pain
fancy (1) imagination (2) whim (3) love
Dutchman, Frenchman . . . see page 176
slops loose baggy breeches

ACT 3   SCENE 2
Leonato's house

Enter DON PEDRO, CLAUDIO, BENEDICK and LEONATO

DON PEDRO I do but stay till your marriage be consummate, and then
    go I toward Arragon.

CLAUDIO I'll bring you thither, my lord, if you'll vouchsafe me.

DON PEDRO Nay that would be as great a soil in the new gloss of your
    marriage, as to show a child his new coat and forbid him to wear it: I   5
    will only be bold with Benedick for his company, for from the crown
    of his head, to the sole of his foot, he is all mirth: he hath twice or
    thrice cut Cupid's bow-string, and the little hangman dare not shoot
    at him: he hath a heart as sound as a bell, and his tongue is the
    clapper, for what his heart thinks, his tongue speaks.   10

BENEDICK Gallants, I am not as I have been.

LEONATO So say I, methinks you are sadder.

CLAUDIO I hope he be in love.

DON PEDRO Hang him, truant, there's no true drop of blood in him to
    be truly touched with love: if he be sad, he wants money.   15

BENEDICK I have the tooth-ache.

DON PEDRO Draw it.

BENEDICK Hang it.

CLAUDIO You must hang it first, and draw it afterwards.

DON PEDRO What, sigh for the tooth-ache?   20

LEONATO Where is but a humour or a worm.

BENEDICK Well, everyone cannot master a grief, but he that has it.

CLAUDIO Yet say I, he is in love.

DON PEDRO There is no appearance of fancy in him, unless it be a fancy
    that he hath to strange disguises, as to be a Dutchman today, a   25
    Frenchman tomorrow, or in the shape of two countries at once, as a
    German from the waist downward, all slops, and a Spaniard from
    the hip upward, no doublet: unless he have a fancy to this foolery, as
    it appears he hath, he is no fool for fancy, as you would have it
    appear he is.   30

CLAUDIO If he be not in love with some woman, there is no believing
    old signs: a brushes his hat a-mornings, what should that bode?

Benedick's friends continue to joke at his expense. Benedick takes Leonato aside for a private word. Don John interrupts his brother's and Claudio's amusement with an ominous-sounding declaration.

1 What if your friend were in love? (in small groups)

Improvise a scene where you suspect that your friend may be in love and start to tease him/her about it. How many of the things that Benedick's friends tease him for can you also apply to your friend (for example, washing face, moodiness, no sense of humour, visits to hairdressers, wearing make-up, listening to romantic music)?

2 'Stuffed tennis balls'

Tennis balls were stuffed with hair in Elizabethan times. Can you remember one of Beatrice's remarks which might explain why Benedick has shaved off his beard (line 36)?

3 'She shall be buried with her face upwards'

Claudio says that Beatrice 'dies for' Benedick (line 50). 'Dies' was a euphemism for sexual orgasm. So what does Don Pedro mean by his reply?

4 A change of mood (in groups of four)

Someone once commented that whenever Don John appeared he 'felt very much the cool of the evening'. Take parts and read lines 48–69. Make your voices create a sharp change of atmosphere.

Do you think Don Pedro and Claudio's exhilaration at their teasing of Benedick disappears immediately on Don John's entrance or some lines later?

---

civet perfume
paint himself use make-up
For the which . . . him that's what people are saying about him
Nay, but his No, that's just his

lute-string a lute was the instrument for love songs
stops frets on the lute
ill conditions bad habits
hobby-horses buffoons
Good den Good evening

DON PEDRO Hath any man seen him at the barber's?

CLAUDIO No, but the barber's man hath been seen with him, and the old ornament of his cheek hath already stuffed tennis balls. 35

LEONATO Indeed he looks younger than he did, by the loss of a beard.

DON PEDRO Nay, a rubs himself with civet, can you smell him out by that?

CLAUDIO That's as much as to say, the sweet youth's in love.

DON PEDRO The greatest note of it is his melancholy. 40

CLAUDIO And when was he wont to wash his face?

DON PEDRO Yea, or to paint himself? For the which I hear what they say of him.

CLAUDIO Nay but his jesting spirit, which is now crept into a lute-string, and now governed by stops. 45

DON PEDRO Indeed that tells a heavy tale for him: conclude, conclude, he is in love.

CLAUDIO Nay but I know who loves him.

DON PEDRO That would I know too, I warrant one that knows him not.

CLAUDIO Yes, and his ill conditions, and in despite of all, dies for him. 50

DON PEDRO She shall be buried with her face upwards.

BENEDICK Yet is this no charm for the tooth-ache: old signor, walk aside with me, I have studied eight or nine wise words to speak to you, which these hobby-horses must not hear.

[*Exeunt Benedick and Leonato*]

DON PEDRO For my life, to break with him about Beatrice. 55

CLAUDIO 'Tis even so: Hero and Margaret have by this played their parts with Beatrice, and then the two bears will not bite one another when they meet.

Enter DON JOHN *the Bastard*

DON JOHN My lord and brother, God save you.

DON PEDRO Good den, brother. 60

DON JOHN If your leisure served, I would speak with you.

DON PEDRO In private?

DON JOHN If it please you, yet Count Claudio may hear, for what I would speak of, concerns him.

DON PEDRO What's the matter? 65

DON JOHN Means your lordship to be married tomorrow?

DON PEDRO You know he does.

DON JOHN I know not that, when he knows what I know.

CLAUDIO If there be any impediment, I pray you discover it.

Don John claims that he has proof of Hero's infidelity. He invites Claudio and Don Pedro to witness Hero's unfaithful behaviour. They vow to shame her in public if she is proved unchaste.

1 Hear the men's anger (in groups of three)

Take a part each and sit facing each other. Read aloud lines 75–100 looking into each other's eyes. How would you describe the manner in which Don John speaks to the other two?

Read aloud lines 91–100. Sound angry and vengeful. Spit out the consonants (especially the d's, t's and s's). What animal does Don John remind you of as he speaks his final words?

These three men are quickly united in their anger at Hero's 'infidelity'. How do the patterns of their sentences from line 88 onwards emphasise this union of male hostility?

2 What has made the men angry? (in smaller groups)

In the previous scene Hero said in all innocence 'How much an ill word may empoison liking'. Which word has most easily empoisoned Claudio and Don Pedro's liking for Hero?

Whose honour are the men more concerned about, Hero's or Claudio's? (It may help you to read pages 165 and 172 at this point.)

3 'If you dare not trust that you see'

In line 88 Don John seems to be saying 'If you are not prepared to believe the evidence of your own eyes, then you can never say that you know anything'. We know that Claudio and Don Pedro should not believe what they are about to 'see' at Hero's bedroom window. Which other characters have already been deceived by what they have 'noted'?

---

aim better at me judge me better
holp to effect helped to bring
  about
suit ill-spent effort wasted
ill-bestowed misused
circumstances shortened to put it
  briefly

paint out depict in full
warrant proof
bear it coldly control your anger
issue outcome
mischief misfortune

DON JOHN You may think I love you not, let that appear hereafter, and   70
    aim better at me by that I now will manifest, for my brother (I think
    he holds you well, and in dearness of heart) hath holp to effect your
    ensuing marriage: surely suit ill-spent, and labour ill-bestowed.
DON PEDRO Why what's the matter?
DON JOHN I came hither to tell you, and circumstances shortened (for   75
    she has been too long a-talking of), the lady is disloyal.
CLAUDIO Who Hero?
DON JOHN Even she, Leonato's Hero, your Hero, every man's Hero.
CLAUDIO Disloyal?
DON JOHN The word is too good to paint out her wickedness, I could   80
    say she were worse, think you of a worse title, and I will fit her to it:
    wonder not till further warrant: go but with me tonight, you shall see
    her chamber window entered, even the night before her wedding
    day: if you love her, then tomorrow wed her: but it would better fit
    your honour to change your mind.   85
CLAUDIO May this be so?
DON PEDRO I will not think it.
DON JOHN If you dare not trust that you see, confess not that you know:
    if you will follow me, I will show you enough: and when you have
    seen more, and heard more, proceed accordingly.   90
CLAUDIO If I see anything tonight, why I should not marry her tomor-
    row in the congregation, where I should wed, there will I shame her.
DON PEDRO And as I wooed for thee to obtain her, I will join with thee,
    to disgrace her.
DON JOHN I will disparage her no farther, till you are my witnesses: bear   95
    it coldly but till midnight, and let the issue show itself.
DON PEDRO Oh day untowardly turned!
CLAUDIO Oh mischief strangely thwarting!
DON JOHN Oh plague right well prevented! So will you say, when you
    have seen the sequel.   100

                          Exeunt

Dogberry, the Master Constable, and his deputy, Verges, set about appointing a constable to take charge of the Watchmen.

---

1 Enter the clowns (in groups of five)

The scene changes to show another level of Messina society. No sooner has Don John begun his plot, than Shakespeare presents us with the simple, ordinary men whose job it will be to bring the villain and his cronies to justice.

In Shakespeare's day, police duties were carried out by the Watch, whose incompetence was a standing joke with Elizabethan playwrights. Tradition has it that Dogberry was modelled on a real constable who lived at Grendon in Buckinghamshire (on Shakespeare's route from Stratford-upon-Avon to London).

Share out the parts of Dogberry, Verges, Seacoal, Watchman 1 and Watchman 2 and read through lines 1–77 to get a sense of what these men are like.

2 Mangling the language (in small groups)

Dogberry tries to sound impressive, but his efforts only result in a confused jumble of words and ideas. Find one or two sentences or phrases that sound impressive but are really absolute nonsense.

Dogberry's particular talent is for **malapropisms** (mistakenly using one word for another similar word). He says 'desartless' (line 8) when he should say 'deserving'. He also confuses 'allegiance' (line 5), 'by nature' (line 14), 'senseless' (line 19), 'comprehend' (line 21) and 'vagrom' (line 21).

Decide what you think he intends to say, and then devise your own version of lines 1–22 entitled 'Dogberry Corrected', in which Dogberry speaks and the others in the group find ways of correcting his mistakes.

---

it were pity but it would be a pity if
salvation Verges confuses his
  words – he means 'damnation'
give them their charge explain
  their duties

Seacoal . . . good name i.e.
  because coal is one of God's
  blessings
well-favoured good-looking
favour appearance
stand stop

ACT 3 SCENE 3
Near Leonato's house

Enter DOGBERRY *and his partner* VERGES *with* SEACOAL,
WATCHMAN 1, WATCHMAN 2 *and the rest of the Watch*

DOGBERRY Are you good men and true?

VERGES Yea, or else it were pity but they should suffer salvation body
and soul.

DOGBERRY Nay, that were a punishment too good for them, if they
should have any allegiance in them, being chosen for the prince's   5
watch.

VERGES Well, give them their charge, neighbour Dogberry.

DOGBERRY First, who think you the most desartless man to be
constable?

WATCHMAN 1 Hugh Oatcake, sir, or George Seacoal, for they can   10
write and read.

DOGBERRY Come hither, neighbour Seacoal, God hath blessed you
with a good name: to be a well-favoured man, is the gift of Fortune,
but to write and read, comes by nature.

SEACOAL Both which, master constable –   15

DOGBERRY You have: I knew it would be your answer: well, for your
favour, sir, why give God thanks, and make no boast of it, and for
your writing and reading, let that appear when there is no need of
such vanity: you are thought here to be the most senseless and fit
man for the constable of the watch: therefore bear you the lantern: 20
this is your charge, you shall comprehend all vagrom men, you are
to bid any man stand, in the prince's name.

79

Dogberry gives a very muddled account of the duties required of the Watch.
He advises them to avoid trouble wherever possible, and to keep well
clear of criminals.

---

1 'Read all about it!' (in small groups)

List all the crimes in lines 21–77 which might go undetected due to
the sleepiness and ineptitude of the Watch. Add to your list any other
'crime' which you know has taken place that night.

Two of you are newspaper sellers shouting out the news headlines
telling of last night's crimes. The rest are the Watchmen, comment-
ing unofficially on what they were doing when the crimes were
committed.

2 The forces of law and order

The 1988 Royal Shakespeare Company production set the play in the 1950s
on a sunlit terrace with sunbathers, swimming pools and glasses of
champagne. This picture shows the Watch. Identify the characters.

How if a will not stand? What if
  he will not stop?
tolerable he means intolerable
belongs to is the proper thing for
ancient experienced

bills pikes or halberds, weapons
true man honest man
hang a dog animals could be
  charged with offences in the
  sixteenth century

SEACOAL How if a will not stand?

DOGBERRY Why then take no note of him, but let him go, and presently
call the rest of the watch together, and thank God you are rid of a   25
knave.

VERGES If he will not stand when he is bidden, he is none of the prince's
subjects.

DOGBERRY True, and they are to meddle with none but the prince's
subjects: you shall also make no noise in the streets: for, for the   30
watch to babble and to talk, is most tolerable and not to be endured.

WATCHMAN 2 We will rather sleep than talk, we know what belongs to
a watch.

DOGBERRY Why you speak like an ancient and most quiet watchman,
for I cannot see how sleeping should offend: only have a care that   35
your bills be not stolen: well, you are to call at all the alehouses, and
bid those that are drunk get them to bed.

SEACOAL How if they will not?

DOGBERRY Why then let them alone till they are sober: if they make you
not then the better answer, you may say, they are not the men you   40
took them for.

SEACOAL Well, sir.

DOGBERRY If you meet a thief, you may suspect him, by virtue of your
office, to be no true man: and for such kind of men, the less you
meddle or make with them, why the more is for your honesty.   45

SEACOAL If we know him to be a thief, shall we not lay hands on him?

DOGBERRY Truly by your office you may, but I think they that touch
pitch will be defiled: the most peaceable way for you, if you do take a
thief, is, to let him show himself what he is, and steal out of your
company.   50

VERGES You have been always called a merciful man, partner.

DOGBERRY Truly I would not hang a dog by my will, much more a man
who hath any honesty in him.

*After giving more advice, Dogberry and Verges leave. As the Watch make
themselves comfortable on the church bench, Borachio and Conrade
enter, unaware that they are being observed.*

1 Stage the eavesdropping and capture
(in groups of about eight)

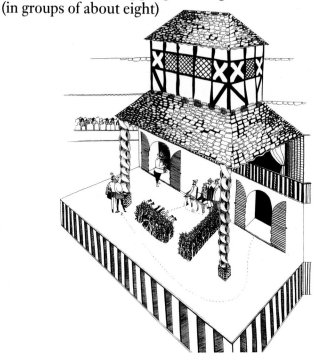

This is an illustration of how the scene might have looked in an
Elizabethan open-air theatre, where no doubt it did sometimes
'drizzle rain' (lines 86–7). Rehearse your version of the moment when
the plot to ruin Hero is overheard (lines 70–147). The Watch can
make the most of their chances to creep around, eavesdrop, whisper,
and drop things.

---

present he means represent
by'r Lady by Our Lady (an oath)
Five . . . on't I bet you five shillings
to one
and there . . . chances if anything
important happens

keep . . . own be discreet
coil hustle and bustle
vigitant he means vigilant
Mass by the Holy Mass (an oath)
scab also means villain
penthouse overhang of roof

VERGES If you hear a child cry in the night, you must call to the nurse
and bid her still it.   55

WATCHMAN 2 How if the nurse be asleep and will not hear us?

DOGBERRY Why then depart in peace, and let the child wake her with
crying, for the ewe that will not hear her lamb when it baas, will
never answer a calf when he bleats.

VERGES 'Tis very true.   60

DOGBERRY This is the end of the charge: you, constable, are to present
the prince's own person, if you meet the prince in the night, you may
stay him.

VERGES Nay by'r Lady that I think a cannot.

DOGBERRY Five shillings to one on't with any man that knows the   65
statutes, he may stay him: marry, not without the prince be willing,
for indeed the watch ought to offend no man, and it is an offence to
stay a man against his will.

VERGES By'r Lady I think it be so.

DOGBERRY Ha, ah ha! Well, masters, good night: and there be any   70
matter of weight chances, call up me: keep your fellows' counsels,
and your own, and good night: come, neighbour.

SEACOAL Well masters, we hear our charge, let us go sit here upon the
church bench till two, and then all to bed.

DOGBERRY One word more, honest neighbours, I pray you watch about   75
Signor Leonato's door, for the wedding being there tomorrow,
there is a great coil tonight: adieu, be vigitant I beseech you.

Exeunt [Dogberry and Verges]

Enter BORACHIO *and* CONRADE

BORACHIO What, Conrade?

SEACOAL Peace, stir not.

BORACHIO Conrade, I say.   80

CONRADE Here, man, I am at thy elbow.

BORACHIO Mass and my elbow itched, I thought there would a scab
follow.

CONRADE I will owe thee an answer for that, and now forward with thy
tale.   85

BORACHIO Stand thee close then under this penthouse, for it drizzles
rain, and I will, like a true drunkard, utter all to thee.

The drunken Borachio starts to tell Conrade about the villainous deed he has done that very night. He then digresses to talk about the influence of fashion on wealthy young gentlemen. The Watch listen, bemused.

1 Fashion and appearance, reality and truth
(in small groups)

Nearly everyone in the play finds it hard to distinguish appearance from reality. The drunken Borachio has just seen how a rich villain (Don John) can simply buy the kind of 'truth' he wants. Now he ponders on the behaviour of the young aristocrats of the day, giddily seeking the latest fashions.

Borachio's words puzzle Conrade. Two of you read lines 89–117. Express Borachio's drunkenness and Conrade's growing exasperation.

a 'What a deformed thief this fashion is'
The remark is said twice and echoed a third time in lines 101–8, so we are meant to 'note' it. Elizabethan fashions, with their padding and strange shapes (see pages 176–7) certainly 'deformed' the human figure. But what other meanings might this remark have? For example, what has fashion or costume 'stolen' from Hero and Benedick? The Watchman is completely foxed. What does *he* think Borachio is talking about?

b 'How giddily a turns about all the hot-bloods'
Late sixteenth-century Elizabethan fashions were elaborate, fantastic and changed with bewildering speed. In lines 109–13, Borachio gives three examples of the kind of costumes that these young 'hot-bloods' copied: Pharoah's soldier, Bel's priest and Hercules. Where does Borachio say each picture may be found?

Find the remark by Conrade which suggests that he, like Borachio, believed that the Elizabethans changed their taste in fashion too easily.

---

stand close keep quiet
be so rich pay so much
make ask
unconfirmed inexperienced, naïve
nothing to a man no indication of
  what the man is really like

a he (as in 'a has' 'a turns')
vane weathervane (what might this
  have to do with fashions?)
reechy dirty, filthy
god Bel a heathen god
cod-piece a man's genital pouch

SEACOAL Some treason, masters, yet stand close.

BORACHIO Therefore know, I have earned of Don John a thousand
ducats. 90

CONRADE Is it possible that any villainy should be so dear?

BORACHIO Thou shouldst rather ask if it were possible any villainy
should be so rich. For when rich villains have need of poor ones,
poor ones may make what price they will.

CONRADE I wonder at it. 95

BORACHIO That shows thou art unconfirmed: thou knowest that the
fashion of a doublet, or a hat, or a cloak, is nothing to a man.

CONRADE Yes, it is apparel.

BORACHIO I mean the fashion.

CONRADE Yes, the fashion is the fashion. 100

BORACHIO Tush, I may as well say the fool's the fool, but seest thou not
what a deformed thief this fashion is?

WATCHMAN 1 I know that Deformed, a has been a vile thief, this seven
year, a goes up and down like a gentleman: I remember his name.

BORACHIO Didst thou not hear somebody? 105

CONRADE No, 'twas the vane on the house.

BORACHIO Seest thou not, I say, what a deformed thief this fashion is,
how giddily a turns about all the hot-bloods, between fourteen and
five and thirty, sometimes fashioning them like Pharaoh's soldiers in
the reechy painting, sometime like god Bel's priests in the old 110
church window, sometime like the shaven Hercules in the smirched
worm-eaten tapestry, where his cod-piece seems as massy as his
club?

CONRADE All this I see, and I see that the fashion wears out more
apparel than the man: but art not thou thyself giddy with the fashion 115
too, that thou hast shifted out of thy tale into telling me of the
fashion?

Borachio tells Conrade the details of how he deceived Don Pedro and
Claudio. The Watch arrest the two villains and lead them away.

1 The villain's story (in groups of about six)

Borachio is drunk and, as he himself admits, tells his tale 'vilely'.
Read lines 118–33 and rehearse a properly ordered version of his
story (it could begin 'I should first tell thee how . . .'). One narrates
while the rest act out the events, perhaps in mime or using improvised
dialogue.

2 How should the villains be arrested?
(in groups of about six)

Rehearse lines 130 (from 'away went Claudio . . .') to the end of the
scene. If you take time to memorise your lines and find some suitable
'weapons', it will be much more effective. Try it in two ways:

- Play it for comedy. The Watch are frightened and incompetent,
  while Borachio and Conrade are drunk and incapable.

- But what if the villains had resisted? Elizabethan gentlemen carried
  swords and often used them. This time the Watch (despite
  Dogberry's advice) should be brave and determined, and the
  villains prepared to fight and kill.

Show both versions to the rest of the class and decide which is the
more appropriate for this scene.

3 Bills and commodities

As they are arrested, Borachio and Conrade find time to make joking
puns on their predicament. 'Bills' were weapons but could also be
credit notes used to buy goods ('commodities'). 'In question' could
either mean 'highly sought after' or 'put on trial'. Why do you think
Borachio and Conrade speak in this way?

---

possessed convinced, evilly
 influenced
o'er night the night before
right honourable, worthy
recovered/lechery he means
 'discovered' and 'treachery'

commonwealth state, country
lock a long curl of hair or lovelock
 (see page 176)
obey you he means 'order'

BORACHIO Not so neither, but know that I have tonight wooed Margaret, the Lady Hero's gentlewoman, by the name of Hero: she leans me out at her mistress' chamber window, bids me a thousand times good night: I tell this tale vilely, I should first tell thee how the prince, Claudio and my master planted, and placed, and possessed, by my master Don John, saw afar off in the orchard this amiable encounter. 120

CONRADE And thought they Margaret was Hero? 125

BORACHIO Two of them did, the prince and Claudio, but the devil my master knew she was Margaret, and partly by his oaths, which first possessed them, partly by the dark night which did deceive them, but chiefly, by my villainy, which did confirm any slander that Don John had made – away went Claudio enraged, swore he would meet her as he was appointed next morning at the temple, and there, before the whole congregation shame her, with what he saw o'er night, and send her home again without a husband. 130

SEACOAL We charge you in the prince's name, stand.

WATCHMAN 2 Call up the right master constable, we have here recovered the most dangerous piece of lechery, that ever was known in the commonwealth. 135

WATCHMAN 1 And one Deformed is one of them, I know him, a wears a lock.

CONRADE Masters, masters. 140

WATCHMAN 1 You'll be made bring Deformed forth I warrant you.

SEACOAL Masters, never speak, we charge you, let us obey you to go with us.

BORACHIO We are like to prove a goodly commodity, being taken up of these men's bills. 145

CONRADE A commodity in question I warrant you: come, we'll obey you.

Exeunt

It is the morning of the wedding and Hero, with Margaret to help her, prepares herself. At first the talk is of fashion, but Margaret turns the conversation to sex.

---

1 Elizabethan ladies' gowns

Portrait of Lady Elizabeth Southwell, a maid of honour to Queen Elizabeth (1599).

Elizabeth's court provided many magnificently rich gowns like this.

The rich fabrics are woven with gold and silver thread ('cloth o' gold'), on which are sewn jewels and pearls. In places there are 'cuts' in the material to show off the contrasting fabrics beneath.

Note the wired neck ruff or 'rebato', the 'tire' (wired head-dress decorated with jewels and false curls), the wide 'down sleeves' and the loose, hanging 'side sleeves'.

The down sleeves and the V-shaped stomacher are heavily padded. The huge skirt is 'round-underborne' (stiffened with material on the inside) and shaped with padding and wire supports.

Read lines 1–18 and decide how closely the Duchess of Milan's and Hero's costumes match this portrait. How do these gowns remind you of something that Borachio said in the previous scene?

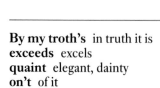

By my troth's in truth it is	**wrest . . . speaking** twist the
exceeds excels	meaning of good words
quaint elegant, dainty	**and it be** if it be
on't of it	**light** can also mean 'immoral'
	else otherwise

ACT 3   SCENE 4
Hero's dressing room

Enter HERO *and* MARGARET *and* URSULA

HERO Good Ursula, wake my cousin Beatrice, and desire her to rise.

URSULA I will, lady.

HERO And bid her come hither.

URSULA Well.   [*Exit*]

MARGARET Troth I think your other rebato were better.   5

HERO No pray thee, good Meg, I'll wear this.

MARGARET By my troth's not so good, and I warrant your cousin will
    say so.

HERO My cousin's a fool, and thou art another, I'll wear none but this.

MARGARET I like the new tire within excellently, if the hair were a   10
    thought browner: and your gown's a most rare fashion i'faith. I saw
    the Duchess of Milan's gown that they praise so.

HERO Oh, that exceeds they say.

MARGARET By my troth's but a night-gown in respect of yours, cloth
    o'gold and cuts, and laced with silver, set with pearls, down sleeves,   15
    side sleeves, and skirts, round underborne with a bluish tinsel – but
    for a fine quaint graceful and excellent fashion, yours is worth ten
    on't.

HERO God give me joy to wear it, for my heart is exceeding heavy.

MARGARET 'Twill be heavier soon by the weight of a man.   20

HERO Fie upon thee, art not ashamed?

MARGARET Of what, lady? Of speaking honourably? Is not marriage
    honourable in a beggar? Is not your lord honourable without mar-
    riage? I think you would have me say, saving your reverence, a
    husband: and bad thinking do not wrest true speaking, I'll offend   25
    nobody: is there any harm in the heavier for a husband? None I
    think, and it be the right husband, and the right wife, otherwise 'tis
    light and not heavy: ask my Lady Beatrice else, here she comes.

*Beatrice enters suffering from a heavy cold. Margaret hints very pointedly
that Beatrice is out of sorts because of her love for Benedick.*

---

1 Tease Beatrice (in groups of about six)

Just as love has given Benedick toothache, it has now given Beatrice a
cold. Three of you read lines 29–74. The rest echo Margaret's words
to Beatrice in a teasing manner.

2 Quick-witted women (in small groups)

Look at the word-play between Margaret and Beatrice in lines 32–7:

Light o'Love was a popular dance song of the day. It means 'the joy
of love'. The tune survives, but not the words. Write your own lyrics
for a song with this title. Can you link the words in some way to the
events in the play (as Balthasar's song does in 2.3.53)?

Margaret claims to want Beatrice to sing this song because it 'goes
without a burden' (i.e. needs no bass or male accompaniment). This,
of course, continues the pun on 'lightness', because 'light o'love'
could also refer to a loose woman. Beatrice takes up the hint with her
use of 'heels' and 'barns'. Kicking up your heels suggested unchastity,
while 'barns' puns on 'bairns' (children). What other sexual innuendoes can you find in the script opposite?

3 'Carduus benedictus'

The Latin name for Holy Thistle (line 60), a popular and fashionable
remedy for many complaints, especially 'perilous diseases of the
heart'. Draw Margaret and Beatrice's faces as lines 54–5 are spoken,
with thought bubbles showing what is on each woman's mind.

Clap's into let us strike up
heigh ho a sigh ('heigh') was also a
 cry used in hawking and riding
H (i.e. 'ache' which was sometimes
 pronounced 'aitch')
and . . . Turk if you have changed
 your beliefs (about love)

star Pole (or fixed) Star
trow I wonder
stuffed blocked nose, or pregnant
apprehension wit
cap i.e. your fool's cap
qualm sudden sickness

Enter BEATRICE

HERO Good morrow, coz.

BEATRICE Good morrow, sweet Hero.   30

HERO Why how now? Do you speak in the sick tune?

BEATRICE I am out of all other tune, methinks.

MARGARET Clap's into *Light o'Love*: that goes without a burden: do you
    sing it and I'll dance it.

BEATRICE Ye light o'love with your heels, then if your husband have   35
    stables enough, you'll see he shall lack no barns.

MARGARET Oh illegitimate construction! I scorn that with my heels.

BEATRICE 'Tis almost five o'clock, cousin, 'tis time you were ready: by
    my troth I am exceeding ill, heigh ho.

MARGARET For a hawk, a horse, or a husband?   40

BEATRICE For the letter that begins them all, H.

MARGARET Well, and you be not turned Turk, there's no more sailing
    by the star.

BEATRICE What means the fool, trow?

MARGARET Nothing I, but God send everyone their heart's desire.   45

HERO These gloves the count sent me, they are an excellent perfume.

BEATRICE I am stuffed, cousin, I cannot smell.

MARGARET A maid and stuffed! There's goodly catching of cold.

BEATRICE Oh God help me, God help me, how long have you pro-
    fessed apprehension?   50

MARGARET Ever since you left it: doth not my wit become me rarely?

BEATRICE It is not seen enough, you should wear it in your cap: by my
    troth I am sick.

MARGARET Get you some of this distilled *Carduus benedictus*, and lay it
    to your heart, it is the only thing for a qualm.   55

HERO There thou prick'st her with a thistle.

BEATRICE *Benedictus*, why *benedictus*? You have some moral in this
    benedictus.

Margaret chatters to Beatrice about love and Benedick. Ursula returns with the news that the men have arrived to take Hero to the church.

---

1 Thoughts before the wedding (in small groups)

Talk about the different moods and attitudes to marriage expressed by Hero, Beatrice and Margaret in this scene.

How closely do the facial expressions of these women match your conclusions?

2 Your thoughts about Margaret (in groups of three)

This young woman, who has unwittingly helped to dishonour her mistress, is not a lowly servant, but neither is she the social equal of Hero or Beatrice.

Margaret uses the respectful 'you' to address Hero while Hero uses 'thou/thee' to signal Margaret's inferior status. Read page 165 and decide why Beatrice should use both 'you' and 'thy' to address Margaret.

Take it in turns to talk to Beatrice (lines 54–70). Try pausing for breath only when you meet a colon or full stop. Which four words or phrases best sum up Margaret's personality?

---

list please, wish
eats ... grudging accepts his destiny (of getting married) without complaint

Not a false gallop I speak the truth (a false gallop, or canter, is not a natural pace for a horse)

MARGARET Moral? No by my troth, I have no moral meaning, I meant
plain Holy Thistle, you may think perchance that I think you are in   60
love, nay by'r Lady I am not such a fool to think what I list, nor I list
not to think what I can, nor indeed I cannot think, if I would think
my heart out of thinking, that you are in love, or that you will be in
love, or that you can be in love: yet Benedick was such another, and
now is he become a man, he swore he would never marry, and yet   65
now in despite of his heart he eats his meat without grudging, and
how you may be converted I know not, but methinks you look with
your eyes as other women do.
BEATRICE What pace is this that thy tongue keeps?
MARGARET Not a false gallop.   70

Enter URSULA

URSULA Madam, withdraw, the prince, the count, Signor Benedick,
Don John, and all the gallants of the town are come to fetch you to
church.
HERO Help to dress me, good coz, good Meg, good Ursula.

[*Exeunt*]

Leonato is busy with the last-minute preparations for the wedding.
Dogberry and Verges come to inform him of the arrest of Borachio and
Conrade, but their ramblings exasperate the impatient Leonato.

1 Don't interrupt me now (in groups of three)

In his anxiety to get to the wedding, Leonato is ironically unaware of
the importance of this interview. For their part, Dogberry and Verges
are equally unaware of how vital their news is.

Take a part each (ignore lines 42–4) and read the scene through.
Dogberry and Verges should be very rambling and 'tedious'. Leonato
should be flustered, irritable and anxious to leave. Can you decide
where Dogberry talks to Leonato and where he talks to Verges?

2 Another ten words bite the dust (in small groups)

It is not easy to insult Dogberry. Leonato tells him that he is 'tedious'
(line 14). Dogberry thinks 'tedious' means 'rich' and very charitably
says that if he *were* rich he would gladly give all his 'tediousness' to
Leonato!

Dogberry misuses and mangles at least another ten words in this
scene. Make a list of these words and say which words you think he
actually meant to use. Join with another group and compare lists.

Headborough Deputy Constable
nearly closely
Goodman title used of a man who
  was below the rank of gentleman
palabras perhaps from 'pocas
  palabras', Spanish for 'few words',

this may be one of the few learned
words that Dogberry gets right!
of your worship on your worship
exclamation on loud complaint
  about
fain know appreciate knowing

ACT 3   SCENE 5
The hall of Leonato's house

Enter LEONATO *and* DOGBERRY *the Constable and* VERGES *the*
Headborough

LEONATO What would you with me, honest neighbour?

DOGBERRY Marry, sir, I would have some confidence with you, that
decerns you nearly.

LEONATO Brief I pray you, for you see it is a busy time with me.

DOGBERRY Marry this it is, sir.   5

VERGES Yes in truth it is, sir.

LEONATO What is it, my good friends?

DOGBERRY Goodman Verges, sir, speaks a little off the matter, an old
man, sir, and his wits are not so blunt, as God help I would desire
they were, but in faith honest, as the skin between his brows.   10

VERGES Yes I thank God, I am honest as any man living, that is an old
man, and no honester than I.

DOGBERRY Comparisons are odorous, palabras, neighbour Verges.

LEONATO Neighbours, you are tedious.

DOGBERRY It pleases your worship to say so, but we are the poor duke's   15
officers, but truly for mine own part, if I were as tedious as a king, I
could find in my heart to bestow it all of your worship.

LEONATO All thy tediousness on me, ah?

DOGBERRY Yea, and 'twere a thousand pound more than 'tis, for I hear
as good exclamation on your worship as of any man in the city, and   20
though I be but a poor man, I am glad to hear it.

VERGES And so am I.

LEONATO I would fain know what you have to say.

Leonato cannot wait for Dogberry to get to the point. He instructs Dogberry to conduct the trial himself, not realising the significance of the crime that has been uncovered.

1 How does Dogberry say it? (in groups of three)

Take the parts of Dogberry, Verges and Leonato. Create your own 'still photographs' (or frozen moments) for the following lines. Hold each freeze for about thirty seconds so that the rest of the class can guess which line you are showing.

'and two men ride . . . behind' (lines 28–9)
'Gifts that God gives' (line 33)
'It shall be suffigance' (line 40)

Dogberry has a high opinion of his own intelligence. Where do you think he points when he says 'here's that shall drive some of them to a noncome' (lines 49–50)?

2 Who's who?

Is this how you imagined these three men might look?

Find the line in this scene which suggests that Dogberry is a much larger man than Verges.

ha' ta'en have arrested	**stay for you** wait for you
arrant out-and-out	**Francis Seacoal** does Shakespeare
world wonder	mean George Seacoal of 3.3?
and two . . . horse if two men ride	**noncome** out of their wits
on one horse (i.e. there can only be	**only** just
one leader)	

VERGES Marry, sir, our watch tonight, excepting your worship's presence, ha' ta'en a couple of as arrant knaves as any in Messina.   25

DOGBERRY A good old man, sir, he will be talking as they say, when the age is in, the wit is out, God help us, it is a world to see: well said i'faith, neighbour Verges, well, God's a good man, and two men ride of a horse, one must ride behind, an honest soul i'faith, sir, by my troth he is, as ever broke bread, but God is to be worshipped, all   30
men are not alike, alas, good neighbour.

LEONATO Indeed, neighbour, he comes too short of you.

DOGBERRY Gifts that God gives.

LEONATO I must leave you.

DOGBERRY One word, sir, our watch, sir, have indeed comprehended   35
two aspitious persons, and we would have them this morning examined before your worship.

LEONATO Take their examination yourself, and bring it me, I am now in great haste, as it may appear unto you.

DOGBERRY It shall be suffigance.   40

[Enter MESSENGER]

LEONATO Drink some wine ere you go: fare you well.

MESSENGER My lord, they stay for you, to give your daughter to her husband.

LEONATO I'll wait upon them, I am ready.

Exit [Leonato with Messenger]

DOGBERRY Go, good partner, go get you to Francis Seacoal, bid him   45
bring his pen and ink-horn to the gaol: we are now to examination these men.

VERGES And we must do it wisely.

DOGBERRY We will spare for no wit I warrant you: here's that shall drive some of them to a noncome, only get the learned writer to set down   50
our excommunication, and meet me at the gaol.

Exeunt

Looking back at Act 3

1 Dark and light (in groups of six or more)

The shifts from comedy to potential tragedy are becoming clearer. Present a five-minute version of Act 3. Speed up the comic moments and make the threatening or serious moments seem slow and intense.

2 Beatrice's thoughts

Act out Beatrice's dream on the night before Hero's wedding. Think about how her subconscious mind might explore Hero's 'criticism' of her (3.1.47–56), as well as her feelings for Benedick.

3 Two friends, two lovers

The two friends, Claudio and Benedick, are also in love with the two main female characters. Write notes on Benedick's love story, then do the same for Claudio.

Compare the stories and the behaviour of the two. Which man feels love more deeply and sincerely? Which man do you find the more attractive and likeable?

4 Just listen to this! (in pairs)

After Act 3 Scene 1 Ursula returns to Margaret to tell her all about what happened in the 'pleachèd bower'. Improvise the dialogue between the two.

5 Men's talk and women's talk (in small groups)

Extend Act 3 Scene 2. Improvise a two-minute exchange between Claudio and Don Pedro which takes place after Don John has left. Show Claudio's anger, resentment and wounded pride. Show as clearly as you can what you think these men are most worried about.

Present a two-minute version of Act 3 Scene 4. Show the women's optimism, teasing and mutual concern as they prepare for Hero's wedding. Don't forget there are also moments of foreboding. What are the women's main concerns?

After watching the other groups' presentations of 'men together' and 'women together', talk together about the differences you have noticed.

6 Headlines

Write newspaper headlines to catch the main action of each scene in Act 3. One headline per scene.

7 The Watch

Jot down as many reasons as you can for the Watch being in the play. Dogberry and his men did not feature at all in Acts 1 and 2. Why should they now suddenly play such a prominent part in events?

Draw a cartoon strip entitled 'Mr Malaprop's Advice'. This should highlight Dogberry's amazing ability to mangle language. *Note*: Mrs Malaprop is a character in Sheridan's play *The Rivals* who muddles up her language.

One student's version of Mr Dogberry Malaprop.

8 Opinion polls (in small groups)

Carry out a survey in your group of the five most sympathetic characters in the play and the five most disliked. Draw up your lists in order of rank. Ask those you interview to give reasons for their choices. Present your findings to the class.

9 Tease the melancholy lovers (in small groups)

Claudio and Don Pedro enjoy teasing Benedick the lover about his 'toothache' (3.2.16–54). Likewise, Margaret enjoys herself with jokes at the expense of the 'sick' Beatrice (3.4).

List your favourite jokes and insults directed at Benedick. Write a similar list for Beatrice. Use your favourite extracts to act out:

- a one-minute teasing of Benedick
- a one-minute teasing of Beatrice.

At the end of each scene, ask the lover how he/she feels. Talk about whether there is any difference between the teasing of Beatrice and the teasing of Benedick.

The guests assemble for the wedding of Hero and Claudio. As Friar Francis begins the marriage ceremony, Claudio refuses to accept Hero as his bride and hands her back to Leonato.

1 'Take her back again' (in large groups)

In Shakespeare's time, marriages among the gentry were arranged as family bargains, and an unchaste bride was a worthless thing (see page 172). Several times, with bitter irony, Claudio calls Hero a 'maid'.

Rehearse your version of lines 1–24. Create a happy and holy occasion as the wedding guests assemble, then a contrast as Claudio begins his denunciation of Hero. Think about Leonato's behaviour as father of the bride and the possible reasons for Benedick's strange interruption. Just how does Claudio return Hero to her father?

2 'Tis pity she's a whore' (in large groups)

Take lines 25–56. As a group, express your reactions to Claudio's accusations in the following ways:

Disbelief Claudio speaks his lines face to face with Hero. The rest act as family and friends. Echo the words and phrases you find unbelievable. At the end ask Hero to say what she is thinking.

Support Repeat the exercise, but now the group members (like Don Pedro) are supporters of Claudio and echo words which emphasise Claudio's anger and disgust. At the end ask Hero how she feels.

2 'This rotten orange' (in pairs)

Why should Claudio choose this phrase to describe Hero? Write it down and, as you read on, write other words and phrases around it from lines 1–104 which are connected in some way to the image of a rotten orange.

---

inward secret
Stand thee by stand to one side
unconstrainèd unforced
counterpoise be of equal weight
render her give her back

learn me teach me
maid innocent virgin
what . . . truth what appearance of authority and truth
withal with

ACT 4   SCENE 1
A church

Enter DON PEDRO, DON JOHN, LEONATO, FRIAR FRANCIS, CLAUDIO,
BENEDICK, HERO and BEATRICE; Wedding Guests

LEONATO Come, Friar Francis, be brief, only to the plain form of
marriage, and you shall recount their particular duties afterwards.

FRIAR FRANCIS You come hither, my lord, to marry this lady?

CLAUDIO No.

LEONATO To be married to her: friar, you come to marry her.   5

FRIAR FRANCIS Lady, you come hither to be married to this count?

HERO I do.

FRIAR FRANCIS If either of you know any inward impediment why you
should not be conjoined, I charge you on your souls to utter it.

CLAUDIO Know you any, Hero?   10

HERO None, my lord.

FRIAR FRANCIS Know you any, count?

LEONATO I dare make his answer, none.

CLAUDIO Oh what men dare do! What men may do! What men daily
do, not knowing what they do!   15

BENEDICK How now! Interjections? Why then, some be of laughing, as,
ah, ha, he.

CLAUDIO Stand thee by, friar: father, by your leave,
　　　Will you with free and unconstrainèd soul
　　　Give me this maid your daughter?   20

LEONATO As freely, son, as God did give her me.

CLAUDIO And what have I to give you back, whose worth
　　　May counterpoise this rich and precious gift?

DON PEDRO Nothing, unless you render her again.

CLAUDIO Sweet prince, you learn me noble thankfulness: 25
　　　There, Leonato, take her back again,
　　　Give not this rotten orange to your friend,
　　　She's but the sign and semblance of her honour:
　　　Behold how like a maid she blushes here!
　　　Oh what authority and show of truth   30
　　　Can cunning sin cover itself withal!

*Claudio declares that he will not marry Hero. Leonato assumes that Hero
has lost her virginity to Claudio, but Claudio denies this. Don Pedro
denounces Hero as a common prostitute.*

1 Inside the villain's head! (in groups of about six)

Don John's plan is going well. He must be delighted to watch such
men of honour denouncing Hero. Read lines 18–88 and work out
what the villain might be thinking at each stage of the events.

Act out these lines with two of you voicing the villainous thoughts
of Don John as he enjoys his success. How does Claudio speak his
lines – is he anguished, angry or pompous? How does Benedick say
line 62 – is he embarrassed, wise-cracking, mumbling, aghast or
cynical?

2 Who's who?

Don John claims to 'know' the truth (line 61). Hero is unchaste. What
do the others present 'know' or believe they 'know'?

- Who's who in the picture?
- Who knows what is true, and who believes what *seems* to be true?
- Talk about what these characters might be thinking.

---

luxurious lustful
approvèd wanton proven whore
known had sex with
extenuate . . . sin find an excuse
  for my sin of taking her virginity
large improper
comely appropriate, fitting

Dian Diana, the cool goddess of the
  moon and of chastity
blown come into full bloom
Venus goddess of love
wide mistakenly, wide of the mark
stale prostitute

Comes not that blood, as modest evidence,
To witness simple virtue? Would you not swear
All you that see her, that she were a maid,
By these exterior shows? But she is none: 35
She knows the heat of a luxurious bed:
Her blush is guiltiness, not modesty.
LEONATO What do you mean, my lord?
CLAUDIO   Not to be married,
Not to knit my soul to an approvèd wanton.
LEONATO Dear my lord, if you in your own proof,   40
Have vanquished the resistance of her youth,
And made defeat of her virginity –
CLAUDIO I know what you would say: if I have known her,
You will say, she did embrace me as a husband,
And so extenuate the forehand sin: no, Leonato,   45
I never tempted her with word too large,
But as a brother to his sister, showed
Bashful sincerity, and comely love.
HERO And seemed I ever otherwise to you?
CLAUDIO Out on thee seeming, I will write against it!   50
You seem to me as Dian in her orb,
As chaste as is the bud ere it be blown:
But you are more intemperate in your blood,
Than Venus, or those pampered animals,
That rage in savage sensuality.   55
HERO Is my lord well, that he doth speak so wide?
LEONATO Sweet prince, why speak not you?
DON PEDRO   What should I speak?
I stand dishonoured that have gone about
To link my dear friend to a common stale.
LEONATO Are these things spoken, or do I but dream?   60
DON JOHN Sir, they are spoken, and these things are true.
BENEDICK This looks not like a nuptial.
HERO   True, oh God!
CLAUDIO Leonato, stand I here?
Is this the prince? Is this the prince's brother?
Is this face Hero's? Are our eyes our own?   65
LEONATO All this is so, but what of this, my lord?

Claudio questions Hero about the man he saw at her window. Hero denies there was a man. Don Pedro and his brother confirm Claudio's accusation of Hero's disloyalty.

1 'Oh God defend me, how am I beset!' (in groups of five)

Take a part each, stand in a circle and slowly read aloud lines 63–92. Use gesture, movement or pointing to emphasise relevant words. Here's an example using Claudio's words in line 67:

> 'Let me (*point to self*) but move one question (*gesture*) to your (*point to Leonato*) daughter (*point to Hero*)'.

Show how the men, including her own father, unite against Hero.

2 'Answer truly to your name' (in pairs)

Hero asks Claudio why she is being questioned (line 72) and claims that her name has no stain upon it. In Greek legend, Hero was the true love of Leander who drowned whilst swimming across the Hellespont to meet her. She in turn drowned herself for love of him. In Shakespeare's time, the name Hero would have suggested faithfulness in love.

Using this legend and what is said in lines 63–101, write a dialogue between Claudio and Hero in which each speaks what they 'know' to be the truth about Hero (both the name and the person).

3 Claudio's farewell (in small groups)

Read aloud lines 93–101 several times. How many examples of word patterns and word-play can you find? Look especially for **oxymorons** (two contradictory ideas placed side by side). For example, talk about Claudio's use of pure/impure and pious/impious contrasts.

What do you think of Claudio as he says farewell to his former bride?

---

kindly power natural authority
catechising questioning (the first question in the Christian Catechism is 'what is your name?')
Hero itself the very name Hero (which he had heard Borachio speak)

liberal gross, coarse
much misgovernment most serious misconduct
conjecture suspicion
never . . . gracious it (beauty) will never again be pleasing

CLAUDIO Let me but move one question to your daughter,
       And by that fatherly and kindly power,
       That you have in her, bid her answer truly.
LEONATO I charge thee do so, as thou art my child.   70
HERO Oh God defend me, how am I beset!
       What kind of catechising call you this?
CLAUDIO To make you answer truly to your name.
HERO Is it not Hero? Who can blot that name
       With any just reproach?
CLAUDIO   Marry that can Hero,   75
       Hero itself can blot out Hero's virtue.
       What man was he, talked with you yesternight,
       Out at your window betwixt twelve and one?
       Now if you are a maid, answer to this.
HERO I talked with no man at that hour, my lord.   80
DON PEDRO Why then are you no maiden. Leonato,
       I am sorry you must hear: upon mine honour,
       Myself, my brother, and this grievèd count
       Did see her, hear her, at that hour last night,
       Talk with a ruffian at her chamber window,   85
       Who hath indeed most like a liberal villain,
       Confessed the vile encounters they have had
       A thousand times in secret.
DON JOHN   Fie, fie, they are
       Not to be named my lord, not to be spoke of,
       There is not chastity enough in language,   90
       Without offence to utter them: thus, pretty lady,
       I am sorry for thy much misgovernment.
CLAUDIO Oh Hero! What a hero hadst thou been,
       If half thy outward graces had been placed
       About thy thoughts and counsels of thy heart?   95
       But fare thee well, most foul, most fair, farewell
       Thou pure impiety, and impious purity,
       For thee I'll lock up all the gates of love,
       And on my eyelids shall conjecture hang,
       To turn all beauty into thoughts of harm,   100
       And never shall it more be gracious.
LEONATO Hath no man's dagger here a point for me?
               [*Hero faints*]

*Don John claims that Hero fainted because her misdeeds have been revealed.
Don Pedro, Don John and Claudio leave. Beatrice fears Hero is dead.
Leonato wishes her dead and regrets he ever had a daughter.*

---

1 Why stay? (in pairs)

This is a crucial moment of decision for Benedick. Should he leave with his friends or stay?

- List the reasons why Benedick might be tempted to leave.
- List his reasons for staying.
- Use this information to present a 'duologue' in which the two halves of Benedick's mind explain his dilemma and his decision.

2 Father and daughter (in large groups or whole class)

Leonato's feelings are intense. He reflects upon the love and pride he felt for Hero and the shame he feels now that her honour 'is fallen into a pit of ink'.

One of you is Hero, one Leonato. Sit Hero on a chair. Leonato and the rest of the group circle Hero. As Leonato addresses his daughter with lines 113–36, the group should violently and angrily echo the 'accusing' words.

Leonato sits facing Hero. As Leonato slowly reads the lines, the group echoes the personal words and phrases (for example, 'I, me, mine'), while Hero repeats the words and phrases that refer to her (for example, 'her, she, thou, Hero'). Then ask Hero to express her thoughts at this moment.

Talk about the emotions being expressed or silently felt. Other fathers in Shakespeare's plays are equally harsh towards their daughters. Compare these lines with *Romeo and Juliet* 3.5.140–95 where Juliet's father tells her what he thinks of her when she refuses to marry Count Paris.

---

how now what's the matter?
spirits vital powers, life force
printed ... blood (1) revealed by her blushes (2) part of her nature
on ... reproaches immediately after reproaching you

Chid ... frame? Did I blame nature for giving me only one child?
issue child, offspring
smirchèd stained
mired muddied
salt ... season meat was salted to prevent it going bad

BEATRICE Why how now, cousin, wherefore sink you down?
DON JOHN Come let us go: these things come thus to light,
     Smother her spirits up.
              [*Exeunt Don Pedro, Don John and Claudio*]
BENEDICK   How doth the lady?   105
BEATRICE Dead I think, help, uncle!
     Hero, why Hero: uncle: Signor Benedick: friar!
LEONATO Oh Fate! Take not away thy heavy hand,
     Death is the fairest cover for her shame
     That may be wished for.
BEATRICE   How now, cousin Hero?   110
FRIAR FRANCIS Have comfort, lady.
LEONATO   Dost thou look up?
FRIAR FRANCIS Yea, wherefore should she not?
LEONATO Wherefore? Why doth not every earthly thing
     Cry shame upon her? Could she here deny
     The story that is printed in her blood?   115
     Do not live, Hero, do not ope thine eyes:
     For did I think thou wouldst not quickly die,
     Thought I thy spirits were stronger than thy shames,
     Myself would on the rearward of reproaches
     Strike at thy life. Grieved I, I had but one?   120
     Chid I for that at frugal nature's frame?
     Oh one too much by thee! Why had I one?
     Why ever wast thou lovely in my eyes?
     Why had I not with charitable hand,
     Took up a beggar's issue at my gates,   125
     Who smirchèd thus, and mired with infamy,
     I might have said, no part of it is mine,
     This shame derives itself from unknown loins:
     But mine, and mine I loved, and mine I praised,
     And mine that I was proud on, mine so much,   130
     That I myself, was to myself not mine,
     Valuing of her: why she, oh she is fallen
     Into a pit of ink, that the wide sea
     Hath drops too few to wash her clean again,
     And salt too little, which may season give   135
     To her foul tainted flesh.

Benedick asks Beatrice if she kept Hero company that night. When Beatrice says no, Leonato is convinced of his daughter's guilt and wishes her dead. Friar Francis believes Hero is innocent.

1 'By noting of the lady' (in groups of four)

Beatrice trusts Hero and knows in her heart that Hero is innocent. Other characters desperately attempt to 'know' the truth by judging or 'noting' the outward signs. Leonato and Friar Francis are two such people. Split into two pairs:

- *Pair One* is Leonato. As you read lines 113–68, list all the outward signs you have observed in Hero and Claudio. What do these signs lead you to believe?

- *Pair Two* is Friar Francis. List all the outward signs you have observed. What are your conclusions and why should people trust you?

Now come together and debate your findings. If you did not know the real truth, which man would you believe?

---

attired wrapped up
belied falsely accused
given . . . fortune allowed matters
  to go on in this way
apparitions signs, appearances
with experimental seal together
  with my experience of life

warrant . . . book support my
  book-learning
divinity status as a theologian
perjury lying
proper nakedness naked truth

BENEDICK Sir, sir, be patient. For my part I am so attired in wonder, I
    know not what to say.
BEATRICE Oh on my soul my cousin is belied.
BENEDICK Lady, were you her bedfellow last night?   140
BEATRICE No truly not, although until last night,
          I have this twelve month been her bedfellow.
LEONATO Confirmed, confirmed, oh that is stronger made,
          Which was before barred up with ribs of iron.
          Would the two princes lie, and Claudio lie,   145
          Who loved her so, that speaking of her foulness,
          Washed it with tears? Hence from her, let her die.
FRIAR FRANCIS Hear me a little, for I have only been
          Silent so long, and given way unto
          This course of fortune, by noting of the lady.   150
          I have marked
          A thousand blushing apparitions,
          To start into her face, a thousand innocent shames,
          In angel whiteness beat away those blushes,
          And in her eye there hath appeared a fire,   155
          To burn the errors that these princes hold
          Against her maiden truth: call me a fool,
          Trust not my reading, nor my observations,
          Which with experimental seal doth warrant
          The tenure of my book: trust not my age,   160
          My reverence, calling, nor divinity,
          If this sweet lady lie not guiltless here,
          Under some biting error.
LEONATO   Friar, it cannot be,
          Thou seest that all the grace that she hath left,
          Is that she will not add to her damnation   165
          A sin of perjury, she not denies it:
          Why seek'st thou then to cover with excuse,
          That which appears in proper nakedness?

Hero is prepared to suffer torture and death if proven guilty. Benedick begins to suspect his friends have been deceived. Leonato swears revenge if this is true. Friar Francis advises them to pretend that Hero has died.

1 Show their reactions (in groups of five)

The accusations of Claudio and the princes have left everyone in turmoil (see picture below and on previous page).

Devise a tableau ('frozen moment') to illustrate a line or sentence from the script opposite. Show your tableau to the rest of the class. Be prepared to hold the freeze for at least thirty seconds so the others can identify each character and guess the line your group is portraying.

2 'Publish it, that she is dead indeed' (in groups of about six)

Act out the plan that Friar Francis urges Leonato to adopt (lines 194–201). One of you narrates the events which the rest mime. Make sure you show every part of Friar Francis's plan.

---

unmeet improper
misprision misunderstanding
have . . . bent of honour are
  absolutely honourable
frame of plotting
means wealth

reft me robbed me
To quit . . . throughly to settle
  scores fully
mourning ostentation formal
  show of mourning

FRIAR FRANCIS Lady, what man is he you are accused of?
HERO They know that do accuse me, I know none: 170
      If I know more of any man alive
      Than that which maiden modesty doth warrant,
      Let all my sins lack mercy. Oh my father,
      Prove you that any man with me conversed,
      At hours unmeet, or that I yesternight   175
      Maintained the change of words with any creature,
      Refuse me, hate me, torture me to death.
FRIAR FRANCIS There is some strange misprision in the princes.
BENEDICK Two of them have the very bent of honour,
      And if their wisdoms be misled in this,   180
      The practice of it lives in John the bastard,
      Whose spirits toil in frame of villainies.
LEONATO I know not: if they speak but truth of her,
      These hands shall tear her, if they wrong her honour,
      The proudest of them shall well hear of it.   185
      Time hath not yet so dried this blood of mine,
      Nor age so eat up my invention,
      Nor fortune made such havoc of my means,
      Nor my bad life reft me so much of friends,
      But they shall find, awaked in such a kind,   190
      Both strength of limb, and policy of mind,
      Ability in means, and choice of friends,
      To quit me of them throughly.
FRIAR FRANCIS   Pause awhile,
      And let my counsel sway you in this case:
      Your daughter here the princes left for dead,   195
      Let her awhile be secretly kept in,
      And publish it, that she is dead indeed:
      Maintain a mourning ostentation,
      And on your family's old monument
      Hang mournful epitaphs, and do all rites,   200
      That appertain unto a burial.
LEONATO What shall become of this? What will this do?

Friar Francis outlines what he hopes will be the healing effect on Claudio when he hears of Hero's 'death'. If his plan fails, Hero will have to enter a nunnery.

1 'On this travail look for greater birth' (in small groups)

Friar Lawrence in *Romeo and Juliet* devised a desperately dangerous scheme to help the young lovers. Here, Shakespeare again gives the Church the unenviable job of trying to avert tragedy. Friar Francis believes there could be four possible outcomes to his plan:

- The news of Hero's death may make those who accused her feel pity (lines 203–5).
- Hero's death will bring about new life in Claudio's deeper love (lines 206–29).
- Hero's death will cleanse her of her tarnished reputation (lines 230–2).
- If the plan fails, Hero can be sent to a nunnery (lines 233–6).

Read the whole speech aloud, handing on to the next person at each colon or full stop. As each person reads, the rest echo the striking words and phrases. What kind of words have you echoed?

Now choose one of the following:

a Look at lines 206–29 of the Friar Francis's speech. Write down the words and images to do with birth/death. Then look at lines 230–6 and write down the words and images that strike you most strongly. Are these words and images different in any way?

b Improvise! At a party one evening you have a row with your boy/girlfriend who was being too friendly with someone else. The next morning you and your friends are talking very angrily about the incident, when you learn that your boy/girlfriend was killed in an accident shortly after leaving the party. After coping with this news for a few moments, you are then told that the whole story was a hoax. What is your reaction?

---

on this travail from this labour
prize . . . worth do not fully
  appreciate
rack stretch, exaggerate
study of imagination brooding
  thoughts

habit clothes
moving excitingly
liver thought to be the source of
  passion
success the outcome
sort not does not turn out

FRIAR FRANCIS Marry, this well carried, shall on her behalf,
    Change slander to remorse, that is some good,
    But not for that dream I on this strange course,   205
    But on this travail look for greater birth:
    She dying, as it must be so maintained,
    Upon the instant that she was accused,
    Shall be lamented, pitied, and excused
    Of every hearer: for it so falls out,   210
    That what we have, we prize not to the worth,
    Whiles we enjoy it; but being lacked and lost,
    Why then we rack the value, then we find
    The virtue that possession would not show us
    Whiles it was ours: so will it fare with Claudio: 215
    When he shall hear she died upon his words
    Th'idea of her life shall sweetly creep
    Into his study of imagination,
    And every lovely organ of her life,
    Shall come apparelled in more precious habit,   220
    More moving-delicate, and full of life,
    Into the eye and prospect of his soul
    Than when she lived indeed: then shall he mourn,
    If ever love had interest in his liver,
    And wish he had not so accusèd her: 225
    No, though he thought his accusation true:
    Let this be so, and doubt not but success
    Will fashion the event in better shape
    Than I can lay it down in likelihood.
    But if all aim but this be levelled false,   230
    The supposition of the lady's death,
    Will quench the wonder of her infamy.
    And if it sort not well, you may conceal her,
    As best befits her wounded reputation,
    In some reclusive and religious life,   235
    Out of all eyes, tongues, minds and injuries.

Benedick advises Leonato to accept Friar Francis's advice and promises secrecy. Alone with Beatrice, he asks how he can help to prove Hero's innocence and tells Beatrice that he loves her.

1 Hero's exit (in groups of four)

Act out lines 237–47 focusing on Hero. Think about how Friar Francis and Leonato behave towards her, how she responds and how she leaves.

2 Beatrice and Benedick's meeting (in pairs)

A crisis often brings out people's real feelings (you will recall Leonato's treatment of his daughter earlier in this scene). Sit facing each other and read lines 248–316.

a Was Don Pedro right?

Don Pedro thought Beatrice and Benedick's next meeting would be hilarious, but what qualities have they revealed in the crisis? Page 126 shows how one production staged this moment.

b A gentler Beatrice?

Note which phrases show a gentler Beatrice with her defences down and which phrases show the old battling Beatrice with her defences up. Can you see any reasons for Beatrice's change of attitude?

c 'Not yours' says Beatrice in line 258, meaning that it is not

Benedick's duty to defend Hero, even though such a man would earn her love. Why might Beatrice believe that Benedick is not the man to challenge Claudio?

d 'As strange as the thing I know not'

No one is quite sure what Beatrice means by this (line 261). Try out various ways of speaking lines 261–4 and decide what you think she means.

---

inwardness close attachment
deal in this act in this affair
Being that ... grief since I am
  overwhelmed with my grief
presently away let us leave at once

to strange ... cure desperate
  diseases require desperate remedies
but prolonged simply postponed
right her prove her innocence
even straightforward
office task, job

BENEDICK Signor Leonato, let the friar advise you,
          And though you know my inwardness and love
          Is very much unto the prince and Claudio,
          Yet, by mine honour, I will deal in this,   240
          As secretly and justly as your soul
          Should with your body.
LEONATO   Being that I flow in grief,
          The smallest twine may lead me.
FRIAR FRANCIS 'Tis well consented, presently away:
          For to strange sores, strangely they strain the cure: 245
          Come, lady, die to live, this wedding day
          Perhaps is but prolonged: have patience and endure.
                              Exeunt [Friar Francis, Leonato and Hero]
BENEDICK Lady Beatrice, have you wept all this while?
BEATRICE Yea, and I will weep a while longer.
BENEDICK I will not desire that.   250
BEATRICE You have no reason, I do it freely.
BENEDICK Surely I do believe your fair cousin is wronged.
BEATRICE Ah, how much might the man deserve of me that would right
          her!
BENEDICK Is there any way to show such friendship?   255
BEATRICE A very even way, but no such friend.
BENEDICK May a man do it?
BEATRICE It is a man's office, but not yours.
BENEDICK I do love nothing in the world so well as you, is not that
          strange?   260
BEATRICE As strange as the thing I know not: it were as possible for me
          to say, I loved nothing so well as you, but believe me not, and yet I
          lie not, I confess nothing, nor I deny nothing: I am sorry for my
          cousin.

> *Beatrice reluctantly admits that she loves Benedick. He swears he will do anything to prove his love for her, but refuses her order to kill Claudio. Beatrice wishes she were a man so she could take revenge herself.*

1 Sword swallowing (in small groups)

Even the word-play becomes deadly serious. When Benedick swears by his sword (line 265), Beatrice warns him not to 'swear and eat it' (meaning 'do not go back on your oath' or perhaps 'do not eat your sword by getting yourself wounded in combat').

Look at the word-play on this page to do with swearing/protesting love and eating words/swords. Work out how it encourages Beatrice to ask Benedick to kill Claudio. How does your study of this word-play help you decide how Beatrice might say her final sentence (line 295)?

2 Moments of truth (in pairs)

Beatrice risks everything in asking Benedick to challenge Claudio. He in turn risks everything if he accepts. This is no longer a game but a crucial test of love. Try one or more of the following:

a Freeze frames

Create six 'frozen moments' (one for each of lines 278–84) which capture the emotions and intentions of Beatrice and Benedick. Show them in sequence to another pair.

b Find the changing moods

Experiment with different ways of saying each line on this page. Tell your partner to say line 265 in different ways (assertively, fondly, excitedly, and so on). Then switch roles and try line 266. Continue through to line 295. Talk about your findings.

c 'Kill Claudio'

Should he? What do *you* think?

By my sword a gentleman's last resort in the defence of honour
protest (1) swear (2) object
stayed . . . hour given me support at a fortunate moment
Is a not is he not

approved . . . villain proved to be the greatest villain
bear her in hand hide his real intentions
unmitigated
rancour uncontrolled hatred

BENEDICK By my sword, Beatrice, thou lovest me.   265

BEATRICE Do not swear and eat it.

BENEDICK I will swear by it that you love me, and I will make him eat it
that says I love not you.

BEATRICE Will you not eat your word?

BENEDICK With no sauce that can be devised to it: I protest I love thee.   270

BEATRICE Why then God forgive me.

BENEDICK What offence, sweet Beatrice?

BEATRICE You have stayed me in a happy hour, I was about to protest I
loved you.

BENEDICK And do it with all thy heart.   275

BEATRICE I love you with so much of my heart, that none is left to
protest.

BENEDICK Come bid me do anything for thee.

BEATRICE Kill Claudio.

BENEDICK Ha, not for the wide world.   280

BEATRICE You kill me to deny it, farewell.

BENEDICK Tarry, sweet Beatrice.

BEATRICE I am gone, though I am here, there is no love in you, nay, I
pray you let me go.

BENEDICK Beatrice.   285

BEATRICE In faith I will go.

BENEDICK We'll be friends first.

BEATRICE You dare easier be friends with me, than fight with mine
enemy.

BENEDICK Is Claudio thine enemy?   290

BEATRICE Is a not approved in the height a villain, that hath slandered,
scorned, dishonoured my kinswoman? Oh that I were a man! What,
bear her in hand, until they come to take hands, and then with
public accusation, uncovered slander, unmitigated rancour? Oh
God that I were a man! I would eat his heart in the market place.   295

Beatrice despairs of finding a man brave enough to take up her cause. Benedick is convinced by her belief that Hero has been wronged and determines to challenge Claudio.

1 Who's the boss? (in pairs)

Even Beatrice is forced to realise her limitations. Three times in this scene she wishes she were a man, as only a man can challenge Claudio.

See how the initiative moves from Beatrice to Benedick. Place two chairs facing each other. Beatrice stands in front of her chair while Benedick sits on his. Read lines 296–316. At every colon or full stop Benedick must attempt to stand up, but Beatrice must push him down again if she feels angry enough. Decide where Benedick becomes determined enough to push Beatrice onto her chair and take control.

a proper saying a likely story
undone ruined
counties counts (another form of the word)
goodly count a fine accusation
Count Comfect Count Candy

curtsies courtly gestures
trim smooth, insincere, glib
this hand (whose hand does he indicate in line 308? in line 314?)
render . . . account pay dearly for what he has done

BENEDICK Hear me, Beatrice.

BEATRICE Talk with a man out at a window, a proper saying.

BENEDICK Nay, but Beatrice.

BEATRICE Sweet Hero, she is wronged, she is slandered, she is undone.

BENEDICK Beat –   300

BEATRICE Princes and counties! Surely a princely testimony, a goodly
count, Count Comfect, a sweet gallant surely, oh that I were a man
for his sake! Or that I had any friend would be a man for my sake!
But manhood is melted into curtsies, valour into compliment, and
men are only turned into tongue, and trim ones too: he is now as   305
valiant as Hercules, that only tells a lie, and swears it: I cannot be a
man with wishing, therefore I will die a woman with grieving.

BENEDICK Tarry, good Beatrice, by this hand I love thee.

BEATRICE Use it for my love some other way than swearing by it.

BENEDICK Think you in your soul the Count Claudio hath wronged   310
Hero?

BEATRICE Yea, as sure as I have a thought, or a soul.

BENEDICK Enough, I am engaged, I will challenge him. I will kiss your
hand, and so I leave you: by this hand, Claudio shall render me a
dear account: as you hear of me, so think of me: go comfort your   315
cousin, I must say she is dead, and so farewell.

                                                                    [*Exeunt*]

Dogberry, Verges and the sexton take evidence from Borachio and Conrade.
Dogberry commences his blundering cross-examination.

---

1 The majesty of the law (in groups of about eight)

Will the forces of law in the guise of Dogberry and Verges be up to
the task of bringing the truth to light? Set up your magistrate's court.
Act out your version of this all-important examination of the villains.
Points to consider:

- Dogberry's plan to catch out Borachio and Conrade. Work out
  what it is (lines 16–27).
- Which of you ensures that the examination is conducted properly?
- Conrade and Borachio are gentlemen accustomed to the society of
  princes and counts. How do they react to their treatment?

2 How many more words do Dogberry and Verges mangle? (in pairs)

Dogberry gets a word wrong with his very first sentence. He uses
'dissembly' when he really means 'assembly' (in what sense is this a
very thought-provoking mistake?). Find the other malapropisms that
he and Verges use in this scene and work out what they should have
said.

3 The class ladder (in groups of four)

Dogberry calls Borachio 'sirrah', a customary form of address to
inferiors. Take a role each as Conrade, Borachio, Verges and
Dogberry.

- Say where you think you stand on the social ladder in relation to
  the other three.
- Explain why you think you are above, below or equal to the others.
- Say which of the others has the traditional right to call you 'sirrah'.

---

sexton a church official whose
  duties included bell-ringing and
  grave-digging
malefactors offenders, criminals
we hope we believe so

knaves rogues
it . . . shortly it will soon be
  generally believed so
go about with get the better of
in a tale telling the same story

ACT 4   SCENE 2
Messina   A courtroom

Enter the Constables DOGBERRY *and* VERGES *and the* SEXTON *as
Town Clerk in gowns,* CONRADE *and* BORACHIO

DOGBERRY Is our whole dissembly appeared?

VERGES Oh a stool and a cushion for the sexton.

SEXTON Which be the malefactors?

DOGBERRY Marry that am I, and my partner.

VERGES Nay that's certain, we have the exhibition to examine.   5

SEXTON But which are the offenders, that are to be examined? Let them
    come before master constable.

DOGBERRY Yea marry, let them come before me: what is your name,
    friend?

BORACHIO Borachio.   10

DOGBERRY Pray write down Borachio. Yours, sirrah?

CONRADE I am a gentleman, sir, and my name is Conrade.

DOGBERRY Write down Master Gentleman Conrade: masters, do you
    serve God?

BORACHIO ⎫
        ⎬ Yea, sir, we hope.   15
CONRADE ⎭

DOGBERRY Write down, that they hope they serve God: and write God
    first, for God defend but God should go before such villains: mas-
    ters, it is proved already that you are little better than false knaves,
    and it will go near to be thought so shortly: how answer you for
    yourselves?   20

CONRADE Marry, sir, we say we are none.

DOGBERRY A marvellous witty fellow I assure you, but I will go about
    with him: come you hither, sirrah, a word in your ear, sir: I say to
    you, it is thought you are false knaves.

BORACHIO Sir, I say to you, we are none.   25

DOGBERRY Well, stand aside, 'fore God they are both in a tale: have you
    writ down, that they are none?

The sexton instructs Dogberry to summon the Watch, who confirm that they overheard Borachio confess his crime. The sexton reveals that Hero has since died and Don John secretly fled.

1 Is the sexton the real hero of the play? (in groups of five)

Talk about the part the sexton plays in this scene and write the notes you think he would make during these proceedings.

Use your notes to present a mime version of lines 1–55. You are allowed one speaking voice (the sexton's) to narrate the events. The sexton should make his opinions of the other characters clear in his narrative. For example, what would his opinion be of Don John?

2 The villains react (in groups of six)

Focus on how Conrade and Borachio behave as the sexton tells the news of Hero's death and Prince John's sudden departure from Messina (lines 51–5). Form two groups of three:

Group One The two villains react unfeelingly to the news. Show their callous reactions and improvise what they might secretly say to each other.

Group Two A villain with a conscience. In this version Borachio, unlike Conrade, is worried and guilt-stricken by the news. Show this moment and let Borachio explain why he is struck by remorse. Improvise the secret dialogue of Conrade and Borachio after they hear the sexton's news.

---

go not . . . examine you are not going the right way about examining

eftest Dogberry seems to have invented this word! He may mean 'deftest', or do you have a better idea?

flat perjury downright lying
Flat burglary downright theft
by mass by the Christian Mass (a mild oath)

SEXTON Master constable, you go not the way to examine, you must call forth the watch that are their accusers.

DOGBERRY Yea marry, that's the eftest way, let the watch come forth. 30

[*Enter* SEACOAL, WATCHMAN 2 *and the rest of the Watch*]

Masters, I charge you in the prince's name, accuse these men.

SEACOAL This man said, sir, that Don John the prince's brother was a villain.

DOGBERRY Write down, Prince John a villain: why this is flat perjury, to call a prince's brother villain. 35

BORACHIO Master constable.

DOGBERRY Pray thee, fellow, peace, I do not like thy look I promise thee.

SEXTON What heard you him say else?

WATCHMAN 2 Marry that he had received a thousand ducats of Don John, for accusing the Lady Hero wrongfully. 40

DOGBERRY Flat burglary as ever was committed.

VERGES Yea by mass that it is.

SEXTON What else, fellow?

SEACOAL And that Count Claudio did mean upon his words, to disgrace Hero before the whole assembly, and not marry her. 45

DOGBERRY Oh villain! Thou wilt be condemned into everlasting redemption for this.

SEXTON What else?

SEACOAL This is all. 50

SEXTON And this is more, masters, than you can deny: Prince John is this morning secretly stolen away: Hero was in this manner accused, in this very manner refused, and upon the grief of this, suddenly died: master constable, let these men be bound, and brought to Leonato's: I will go before and show him their examination. [*Exit*] 55

As the Watch escort the prisoners away, Conrade offers some resistance. He calls Dogberry an ass, which Dogberry considers to be a terrible insult.

---

1 Dogberry – pompous ass or sad man?
(in large groups or whole class)

The sexton has gone, so there is no one left to record the terrible crime of calling the Master Constable an ass. It is an insult that still annoys Dogberry when next we see him!

a Pompous ass?

Two of you read the parts of Dogberry and Conrade (lines 57–71). When Dogberry speaks, Conrade leads the rest of the group in mockingly echoing what the Master Constable says. Dogberry should be angrily pompous in response to this.

b Sad man?

Decide whether Dogberry deserves some sympathy – some productions have made this an emotional moment. Dogberry talks about financial losses (lines 68–9), and is obviously sensitive about his position and prestige. For example, he boasts about having two gowns (gowns were expensive and a mark of affluence and authority). When Dogberry and Conrade speak lines 57–71, the rest of the group must echo and comment in support of Dogberry, who should respond to their sympathy.

2 Huffing and puffing (in pairs)

You will by now have formed your own picture of Dogberry and Verges.

Choose one character each. Find a short phrase from lines 1–71 which is very typical of your character. Memorise it.

Each pair now gives their physical 'illustration' of these two men as they huff and puff about the room. Switch roles/lines and repeat.

---

opinioned pinioned, bound
coxcomb fool
God's my life a mild oath
naughty wicked, worthless (a much stronger meaning than today)

varlet rogue, low fellow
go to I'll have you know
had been . . . an ass could have been recorded (in writing by the sexton) as an ass

VERGES Come, let them be opinioned.

CONRADE Let them be in the hands of coxcomb.

DOGBERRY God's my life, where's the sexton? Let him write down the
    prince's officer coxcomb: come, bind them, thou naughty varlet.

CONRADE Away, you are an ass, you are an ass.   60

DOGBERRY Dost thou not suspect my place? Dost thou not suspect my
    years? Oh that he were here to write me down an ass! But masters,
    remember that I am an ass, though it be not written down, yet forget
    not that I am an ass: no, thou villain, thou art full of piety as shall be
    proved upon thee by good witness: I am a wise fellow, and which is   65
    more, an officer, and which is more, a householder, and which is
    more, as pretty a piece of flesh as any is in Messina, and one that
    knows the law, go to, and a rich fellow enough, go to, and a fellow
    that hath had losses, and one that hath two gowns, and everything
    handsome about him: bring him away: oh that I had been writ down   70
    an ass!

                                                              Exeunt

Looking back at Act 4

1 Beatrice speaks

Beatrice probably anticipated that the wedding would be a difficult time for her. She had been 'exceeding ill' that morning and faced the prospect of her first meeting with Benedick since learning of his love for her. However, she could not have foreseen the shocks in store for her.

a Quickly note down a chronological list of what happens to Beatrice in Act 4. After each item, write what you think Beatrice is feeling.

b Form a small group and put together a combined list using all your best ideas. Use this to prepare a 'Beatrice-monologue' in which you take turns at telling Beatrice's version of the events at the church. The picture below and those earlier in Act 4 may help you.

c Present your version to the class. Be inventive. Think about how you might share the lines, speak as a chorus, echo, or mime to show her emotions.

Benedick attempts to comfort a distraught Beatrice.

2 Benedick's moments of decision

Benedick is almost as shaken by the events of Act 4 Scene 1 as Beatrice. Devise a way of showing the changes in his emotions, perhaps by means of a graph or chart, or through a series of cartoons with captions. Two of you could show the changes dramatically with one person naming the mood, and the other showing it.

3 Wounded pride

Look back at Dogberry's comic display of wounded pride (4.2.61–71). Claudio's speeches (4.1.25–101) are more serious outpourings of wounded vanity. Look carefully at what both men say. Make notes on:

- what motivates each man to say what he does
- how the language of each man differs
- which of the two men you have more sympathy for, and why.

4 Outward signs and inner truths

Many characters try to judge inner truth by outward signs. Leonato, Don Pedro, Claudio and the Friar have all 'noted' different things about the lady. Leonato 'notes' Claudio's tears (4.1.147), which *he* interprets as a sign of the young man's sincerity. Dogberry lists all the outward signs of his own dignity and wealth (4.2).

Find a way of presenting these ideas about outward signs and inner truths to the class. This might be as a diagram, a comic strip with captions, as columns headed 'Truth' and 'Signs' – or think of your own visual presentation.

5 The silent Hero speaks

Imagine Hero has been placed in a nunnery. There, she gives a frank account of what happened to her at the wedding. What would she say? Have her talk about her hopes before the wedding, what happened at the church, what she now thinks of Claudio, Don Pedro and Leonato, and how she views her present situation.

6 Darts and swords

Draw an outline figure of Claudio as Beatrice might see him. Around this figure write some of the words she has used to describe him, and also the wrongs she thinks he has done. Imagine that you are Beatrice using this figure as a dartboard. Say what you think of Claudio as you throw your imaginary darts. A partner writes down everything you call him!

Antonio attempts to console his brother, but Leonato continues to grieve at the loss of his daughter's reputation and will not be comforted.

---

1 The darkness of grief (in groups of three)

The play has come very close to tragedy. Leonato expresses his feelings of grief (lines 3–32) in three sections:

- Only the man who has loved and suffered can rightfully talk of patience and endurance (lines 3–19).
- But there is no such man. When a man feels grief, all thoughts of patience and endurance are immediately forgotten (lines 20–6).
- All men can preach patience to those who suffer, but no one can practise what they preach when sorrow comes to them (lines 27–32).

Take a section each and practise reading it to yourself with as much anguish as you can. Then come back together and read the lines in sequence telling your partners about your grief.

2 Genuine grief? (in small groups)

Collect about six phrases that Leonato uses to express his grief and talk about how powerful or moving you find them.

Think about what happened at the wedding (4.1) and decide whether Leonato's grief is understandable, or whether he is over-reacting.

---

lineament feature
wag look foolish
cry hem cough uncertainly
make . . . wasters drown sorrow by studying late into the night
preceptial medicine moral instruction
wring writhe with pain
sufficiency ability
advertisement the giving (of advice)

ACT 5   SCENE 1
Outside Leonato's house

Enter LEONATO *and his brother* ANTONIO

ANTONIO If you go on thus, you will kill yourself,
      And 'tis not wisdom thus to second grief,
      Against yourself.
LEONATO   I pray thee cease thy counsel,
      Which falls into mine ears as profitless,
      As water in a sieve: give not me counsel,   5
      Nor let no comforter delight mine ear,
      But such a one whose wrongs do suit with mine.
      Bring me a father that so loved his child,
      Whose joy of her is overwhelmed like mine,
      And bid him speak of patience,   10
      Measure his woe the length and breadth of mine,
      And let it answer every strain for strain,
      As thus for thus, and such a grief for such,
      In every lineament, branch, shape and form:
      If such a one will smile and stroke his beard,   15
      And sorrow; wag, cry hem, when he should groan;
      Patch grief with proverbs, make misfortune drunk
      With candle-wasters: bring him yet to me,
      And I of him will gather patience:
      But there is no such man, for, brother, men   20
      Can counsel and speak comfort to that grief,
      Which they themselves not feel, but tasting it,
      Their counsel turns to passion, which before,
      Would give preceptial medicine to rage,
      Fetter strong madness in a silken thread,   25
      Charm ache with air, and agony with words –
      No, no, 'tis all men's office, to speak patience
      To those that wring under the load of sorrow,
      But no man's virtue nor sufficiency
      To be so moral, when he shall endure   30
      The like himself: therefore give me no counsel,
      My griefs cry louder than advertisement.

As Leonato's mind turns to thoughts of revenge, the sight of Claudio and Don Pedro hurrying past quickly arouses his anger.

---

1 Feelings are running high (in groups of about six)

There are many powerful outbursts in this scene. Present lines 27–57 in a way that highlights the swift changes of mood.

Consider the way in which Leonato and Antonio talk together, the manner of Don Pedro and Claudio's entrance, how each reacts on seeing Leonato, and the response of the two old men. How can you emphasise the meaning of Leonato's remarks in lines 47–57?

2 Philosophers and the toothache (in small groups)

Leonato says in lines 35–8 that philosophers have spoken very dismissively about how hard it is to endure pain and misfortune ('made a push at chance and sufferance'), but when they are put to the test themselves (i.e. when they have to 'endure the tooth-ache'), they can't practise what they preach.

Devise a short scene or draw a cartoon which illustrates the meaning of Leonato's image.

3 Thou/thy and you/your (in pairs)

You will remember how Leonato addressed his guests in the opening scene using the polite 'you' form. Use of the 'thou' form can signal friendship, but it can also imply contempt (see page 165).

Take it in turns to tell Claudio what you think of him (lines 52–7 from 'Who wrongs him?' onwards). Stress all the thee/thou words. Try it in different ways, mockingly, smilingly or angrily. How does all this explain Claudio's actions at line 54?

However however much
writ . . . gods assumed a god-like
  superiority in their writings
bend turn
belied falsely accused

all is one it doesn't matter now
dissembler deceiver
beshrew a curse on
to in moving to

ANTONIO Therein do men from children nothing differ.
LEONATO I pray thee peace, I will be flesh and blood,
   For there was never yet philosopher,   35
   That could endure the tooth-ache patiently,
   However they have writ the style of gods,
   And made a push at chance and sufferance.
ANTONIO Yet bend not all the harm upon yourself,
   Make those that do offend you suffer too.   40
LEONATO There thou speak'st reason, nay I will do so,
   My soul doth tell me, Hero is belied,
   And that shall Claudio know, so shall the prince,
   And all of them that thus dishonour her.

    Enter DON PEDRO *and* CLAUDIO

ANTONIO Here comes the prince and Claudio hastily.   45
DON PEDRO Good den, good den.
CLAUDIO   Good day to both of you.
LEONATO Hear you, my lords?
DON PEDRO   We have some haste, Leonato.
LEONATO Some haste, my lord! Well, fare you well, my lord,
   Are you so hasty now? Well, all is one.
DON PEDRO Nay do not quarrel with us, good old man.   50
ANTONIO If he could right himself with quarrelling,
   Some of us would lie low.
CLAUDIO   Who wrongs him?
LEONATO Marry thou dost wrong me, thou dissembler, thou:
   Nay, never lay thy hand upon thy sword,
   I fear thee not.
CLAUDIO   Marry beshrew my hand,   55
   If it should give your age such cause of fear,
   In faith my hand meant nothing to my sword.

Leonato challenges Claudio to single combat, but Claudio refuses to fight a duel with the old man. Then Antonio challenges Claudio so fiercely that even Leonato is surprised.

1 Challenges (in groups of four)

Stand face to face, Leonato and Antonio versus Claudio and Don Pedro. Read aloud lines 58–90. Gesture vigorously as you speak your lines. Leonato could prod Claudio firmly with his finger on each relevant word (for example, Claudio, thy, thee) and pat his own chest when referring to himself. Make up similarly convincing actions and gestures for Claudio and Antonio.

If you were the director, how would you suggest Don Pedro behaves during all of this?

2 Comedy or tragedy? (in groups of eight)

Split into two companies of four. One company rehearses a comic version of lines 58–107 – the ridiculous sight of two old men challenging a young soldier who has just returned from fighting a war.

You remember Borachio's words to Don John how his plan will 'kill Leonato'? The second company rehearses a serious and tragic version of the same lines – the desperate challenge of a father whose daughter's life has been destroyed, followed by the second challenge of a loyal brother.

Present your versions to each other and talk about the different possibilities of each approach.

---

fleer smile contemptuously
dotard senile old man
to thy head to your face
trial . . . a man single combat
never . . . slept never before has any disgrace been buried

nice fence skilful swordsmanship
lustihood physical fitness
daff me brush me aside
foining thrusting (fencing term)
apes fools
Jacks rogues

LEONATO Tush, tush, man, never fleer and jest at me,
I speak not like a dotard, nor a fool,
As under privilege of age to brag,   60
What I have done, being young, or what would do,
Were I not old: know, Claudio, to thy head,
Thou hast so wronged mine innocent child and me,
That I am forced to lay my reverence by,
And with grey hairs and bruise of many days,   65
Do challenge thee to trial of a man:
I say thou hast belied mine innocent child.
Thy slander hath gone through and through her heart,
And she lies buried with her ancestors:
Oh in a tomb where never scandal slept,   70
Save this of hers, framed by thy villainy.
CLAUDIO My villainy?
LEONATO   Thine, Claudio, thine I say.
DON PEDRO You say not right, old man.
LEONATO   My lord, my lord,
I'll prove it on his body if he dare,
Despite his nice fence, and his active practice,   75
His May of youth, and bloom of lustihood.
CLAUDIO Away, I will not have to do with you.
LEONATO Canst thou so daff me? Thou hast killed my child,
If thou kill'st me, boy, thou shalt kill a man.
ANTONIO He shall kill two of us, and men indeed,   80
But that's no matter, let him kill one first:
Win me and wear me, let him answer me,
Come follow me, boy, come, Sir Boy, come follow me,
Sir Boy, I'll whip you from your foining fence,
Nay, as I am a gentleman, I will.
LEONATO   Brother.   85
ANTONIO Content yourself, God knows, I loved my niece,
And she is dead, slandered to death by villains,
That dare as well answer a man indeed,
As I dare take a serpent by the tongue.
Boys, apes, braggarts, Jacks, milksops.
LEONATO   Brother Anthony.   90

Don Pedro maintains his belief that Claudio was correct in his accusation of Hero. As the two old men depart in anger, a grimly determined Benedick arrives on the scene.

1 'Fashion-monging boys' (in groups of four)

Antonio (lines 91–8) sees Claudio as one of those shallow, worthless fashion-conscious ('fashion-monging') men that Borachio so despises (3.3.107–13). Write a list of equivalent modern insults which an angry old man/woman might hurl at a young man who is too full of himself.

Review Claudio's actions in the play so far. Then two of you make a list of all the criticisms that Antonio and Leonato might level against him. The other two make a list of the things that Claudio might say in defence of his actions. Put your point of view to the other pair and decide which parts of each side's case you can accept.

2 Challenges and threats (in groups of five)

a Antonio's challenge – an old man's rage (lines 91–107)
How much rage and 'ancient fury' can your Antonio summon up? But think also how ludicrous it is for an old man to 'attack' a proven fighter like Claudio. The others will need to consider how they can help convey this combination of fury and ridiculousness.

b Benedick's entrance – a real threat (lines 109–21)
Benedick has also come to challenge Claudio, but his manner is very different from Antonio's. Think about the dramatic pause between the exits and the entrance, how Don Pedro and Claudio react as their friend enters, and how Benedick can convey his determination.

Show your version and talk about the combination of comedy and seriousness.

---

scruple tiniest amount
scambling unruly, arguing
out-facing conceited, swaggering
cog cheat
flout brag

deprave abuse people
Go anticly dress grotesquely
durst cared to go that far
high proof extremely

ANTONIO Hold you content, what, man! I know them, yea
        And what they weigh, even to the utmost scruple:
        Scambling, out-facing, fashion-monging boys,
        That lie, and cog, and flout, deprave and slander,
        Go anticly, and show outward hideousness,   95
        And speak off half a dozen dangerous words,
        How they might hurt their enemies, if they durst,
        And this is all.
LEONATO But brother Anthony –
ANTONIO   Come 'tis no matter,
        Do not you meddle, let me deal in this.   100
DON PEDRO Gentlemen both, we will not wake your patience,
        My heart is sorry for your daughter's death:
        But on my honour she was charged with nothing
        But what was true, and very full of proof.
LEONATO My lord, my lord –
DON PEDRO   I will not hear you.   105
LEONATO No come, brother, away, I will be heard.
ANTONIO And shall, or some of us will smart for it.

                           Exeunt Leonato and Antonio
DON PEDRO See, see, here comes the man we went to seek.

               Enter BENEDICK

CLAUDIO Now, signor, what news?
BENEDICK   Good day, my lord.
DON PEDRO Welcome, signor, you are almost come to part almost a   110
    fray.
CLAUDIO We had like to have had our two noses snapped off with two
    old men without teeth.
DON PEDRO Leonato and his brother: what think'st thou? Had we
    fought, I doubt we should have been too young for them.   115
BENEDICK In a false quarrel there is no true valour: I came to seek you
    both.
CLAUDIO We have been up and down to seek thee, for we are high
    proof melancholy, and would fain have it beaten away, wilt thou use
    thy wit?   120
BENEDICK It is in my scabbard, shall I draw it?

Benedick remains unmoved by Don Pedro and Claudio's light-hearted mockery. He challenges Claudio for bringing about the death of Hero.

1 Attempts at light-heartedness (in groups of three)

Don Pedro and Claudio look to Benedick to cheer them up after their bruising encounter with Leonato and Antonio.

- Benedick's serious reference to his wit being his sword (lines 121–4) is joked about as Claudio asks him to 'draw' his wit just as a minstrel would draw pleasant music from his instrument.
- Benedick then uses the fighting image (lines 129–30) of a 'career' or charge of knights in a tournament. Claudio jokingly counters this by comparing Benedick to a knight who breaks his lance with a clumsy sideways blow ('give him another staff, this last was broke cross').

Take a part each and read lines 118–46. At what point does the joking start to turn sour? Does Claudio realise before Don Pedro?

2 A warning signal (groups of three)

Elizabethans might well have sensed very quickly that all was not right with Benedick. Read page 165 on the use of 'thou/you', then take a part each and read lines 122–56. Stress forcefully every 'thou/thy' and 'you/your'. Who uses which form? What prompts Claudio to change his manner of address during these lines?

3 What does Don Pedro think of all this?

The prince tells Benedick of the witty remarks that Beatrice made about him (lines 147–56). How would you direct Don Pedro to speak these lines, and how would you direct the other two men to react and behave?

---

care . . . cat a proverb
how . . . girdle what to do about it
calf, capon, woodcock all stupid, harmless animals
curiously skilfully
fine (1) very good (2) delicate

wise gentleman fool
hath the tongues speaks several languages
forswore retracted, took back
trans-shape distort
properest most handsome

DON PEDRO Dost thou wear thy wit by thy side?

CLAUDIO Never any did so, though very many have been beside their
    wit: I will bid thee draw, as we do the minstrels, draw to pleasure us.

DON PEDRO As I am an honest man, he looks pale, art thou sick, or   125
    angry?

CLAUDIO What, courage, man: what though care killed a cat, thou hast
    mettle enough in thee to kill care.

BENEDICK Sir, I shall meet your wit in the career, and you charge it
    against me: I pray you choose another subject.   130

CLAUDIO Nay then, give him another staff, this last was broke cross.

DON PEDRO By this light, he changes more and more, I think he be
    angry indeed.

CLAUDIO If he be, he knows how to turn his girdle.

BENEDICK Shall I speak a word in your ear?   135

CLAUDIO God bless me from a challenge.

BENEDICK You are a villain, I jest not, I will make it good how you dare,
    with what you dare, and when you dare: do me right, or I will protest
    your cowardice: you have killed a sweet lady, and her death shall fall
    heavy on you: let me hear from you.   140

CLAUDIO Well I will meet you, so I may have good cheer.

DON PEDRO What, a feast, a feast?

CLAUDIO I'faith I thank him, he hath bid me to a calf's head and a
    capon, the which if I do not carve most curiously, say my knife's
    naught: shall I not find a woodcock too?   145

BENEDICK Sir, your wit ambles well, it goes easily.

DON PEDRO I'll tell thee how Beatrice praised thy wit the other day: I
    said thou hadst a fine wit, true said she, a fine little one: no said I, a
    great wit: right says she, a great gross one: nay said I, a good wit: just
    said she, it hurts nobody: nay said I, the gentleman is wise: certain   150
    said she, a wise gentleman: nay said I, he hath the tongues: that I
    believe said she, for he swore a thing to me on Monday night, which
    he forswore on Tuesday morning, there's a double tongue, there's
    two tongues: thus did she an hour together trans-shape thy particu-
    lar virtues, yet at last she concluded with a sigh, thou wast the   155
    properest man in Italy.

Benedick resigns from Don Pedro's service. He informs the prince that Don John has fled and accuses his former friends of bringing about the death of Hero. Don John's men are brought in under guard.

1 Accusations (in groups of four)

Two of you speak Benedick's parting words (lines 167–73) to the other two, changing over at each colon. Then reverse roles and do it again. Try different ways of accusing your two former friends.

2 'The old man's daughter told us all' (in pairs)

The pressure of events is even getting to Don Pedro. His remark in line 159 surely refers to Hero. What kind of man would make this sort of comment? What do you think of Claudio's reaction to the prince's words?

3 Echoes

Every Shakespeare play is full of resonances. As each scene unfolds, you start to hear echoes of language that has been used before.

a Cuckolds again

In lines 158–66 Don Pedro and Claudio hint at the trick they played on Benedick, and mock him with the cuckolded husband joke. Find the remarks Benedick made in 1.1 which are echoed here when Don Pedro and Claudio talk of the 'savage bull's horns' and 'Benedick the married man'. What is ironic about their jesting here when you consider what has just happened in Acts 3 and 4?

b 'Lord Lack-beard there'

List the insults that Benedick aims at Claudio in this scene. Compare them with the comments Beatrice has made about the Count (2.1.222–4 and 4.1.291–307). Are there any similarities?

---

deadly until she died
braggarts boasters
doublet and hose i.e. his usual
  clothes
giant hero
ape fool

doctor wise man
sad serious
ne'er weigh . . . balance never
  again weigh up the evidence in her
  scales
Hearken after enquire into

CLAUDIO For the which she wept heartily, and said she cared not.

DON PEDRO Yea that she did, but yet for all that, and if she did not hate him deadly, she would love him dearly, the old man's daughter told us all.   160

CLAUDIO All, all, and moreover, God saw him when he was hid in the garden.

DON PEDRO But when shall we set the savage bull's horns on the sensible Benedick's head?

CLAUDIO Yea and text underneath, 'Here dwells Benedick the married   165
man'?

BENEDICK Fare you well, boy, you know my mind, I will leave you now to your gossip-like humour: you break jests as braggarts do their blades, which God be thanked hurt not: my lord, for your many courtesies I thank you: I must discontinue your company: your   170
brother the bastard is fled from Messina: you have among you killed a sweet and innocent lady: for my Lord Lack-beard there, he and I shall meet, and till then peace be with him.   [Exit]

DON PEDRO He is in earnest.

CLAUDIO In most profound earnest, and I'll warrant you, for the love of   175
Beatrice.

DON PEDRO And hath challenged thee?

CLAUDIO Most sincerely.

DON PEDRO What a pretty thing man is, when he goes in his doublet and hose, and leaves off his wit!   180

CLAUDIO He is then a giant to an ape, but then is an ape a doctor to such a man.

DON PEDRO But soft you, let me be, pluck up my heart, and be sad, did he not say my brother was fled?

Enter DOGBERRY *and* VERGES, CONRADE *and* BORACHIO [*with Watchmen*]

DOGBERRY Come you, sir, if justice cannot tame you, she shall ne'er   185
weigh more reasons in her balance, nay, and you be a cursing hypocrite once, you must be looked to.

DON PEDRO How now, two of my brother's men bound? Borachio one.

CLAUDIO Hearken after their offence, my lord.

DON PEDRO Officers, what offence have these men done?   190

As Dogberry begins his repetitive and garbled account of the trial, Don Pedro questions Borachio, who immediately confesses the whole plot to disgrace Hero.

1 Comedy and tragedy (in groups of four)

To explore the mingling of comedy and seriousness, take a part each and read lines 183–224. Decide where the comic element dominates and where the serious. How should Don Pedro and Claudio speak lines 214–5 and why do they speak in blank verse?

2 Borachio's confession (in groups of about eight)

One person takes the part of Borachio, the rest take up the positions of the other characters present, including the Watch.

As Borachio slowly reads lines 203–13, he points to the relevant characters (see page 64 for an example of how to do this). Repeat this with the other characters reacting to and echoing Borachio's words. Present your version to the class.

3 The heart of the play? (in small groups)

Borachio's account of how he deceived Claudio and Don Pedro (lines 203–13) is extremely perceptive. The central preoccupation of the play is the problem of telling truth from illusion, appearance from reality. What comment do the following sentences make about this problem?

- 'I have deceived even your very eyes'
- 'what your wisdoms could not discover, these shallow fools have brought to light'
- 'you . . . saw me court Margaret in Hero's garments'.

---

in his own division divided up in the same way (as Dogberry's speech)
there's . . . suited you've found four ways of saying the same thing

bound . . . answer summoned to answer charges
cunning clever
set thee on urge you
rare semblance exquisite appearance

DOGBERRY Marry, sir, they have committed false report, moreover they
have spoken untruths, secondarily, they are slanders, sixth and
lastly, they have belied a lady, thirdly they have verified unjust
things, and to conclude, they are lying knaves.

DON PEDRO First I ask thee what they have done, thirdly I ask thee   195
what's their offence, sixth and lastly why they are committed, and to
conclude, what you lay to their charge?

CLAUDIO Rightly reasoned, and in his own division, and by my troth
there's one meaning well suited.

DON PEDRO Who have you offended, masters, that you are thus bound   200
to your answer? This learned constable is too cunning to be under-
stood: what's your offence?

BORACHIO Sweet prince, let me go no farther to mine answer: do you
hear me, and let this count kill me: I have deceived even your very
eyes: what your wisdoms could not discover, these shallow fools   205
have brought to light, who in the night overheard me confessing to
this man, how Don John your brother incensed me to slander the
Lady Hero, how you were brought into the orchard, and saw me
court Margaret in Hero's garments, how you disgraced her when
you should marry her: my villainy they have upon record, which I   210
had rather seal with my death, than repeat over to my shame: the
lady is dead upon mine and my master's false accusation: and briefly
I desire nothing but the reward of a villain.

DON PEDRO Runs not this speech like iron through your blood?

CLAUDIO I have drunk poison whiles he uttered it.   215

DON PEDRO But did my brother set thee on to this?

BORACHIO Yea, and paid me richly for the practice of it.

DON PEDRO He is composed and framed of treachery,
    And fled he is upon this villainy.

CLAUDIO Sweet Hero, now thy image doth appear   220
    In the rare semblance that I loved it first.

DOGBERRY Come, bring away the plaintiffs, by this time our sexton hath
reformed Signor Leonato of the matter: and masters, do not forget
to specify when time and place shall serve, that I am an ass.

VERGES Here, here comes Master Signor Leonato, and the sexton too.   225

Leonato returns. Claudio and the prince, full of remorse, beg to be able to make amends. Leonato orders Claudio to mourn Hero's death that night at her tomb and later marry his niece.

1 'And so dies my revenge' (in groups of about eight)

A very thin line divides Shakespearean comedy from tragedy. The outcome of this play could so easily have been different. In *Othello* (a later play), Shakespeare showed just how disastrous it could be when a man suspects his wife of having an affair.

Act out lines 226–60 in a way that shows Leonato's anger and vengeful feelings, but also his forgiveness and mercy. One production even made the audience laugh at line 255. Can you?

Go back to the situation at the end of Act 4 Scene 1 and talk about the different tragic outcomes that the play could easily have had.

2 Points of view

Characters could react to the events in this scene in very different ways. For example, Beatrice might feel very strongly that Claudio does not deserve Leonato's 'kindness'.

Choose one of the following:

- Claudio's diary
- a conversation between Hero and Margaret
- a speech by Beatrice
- a letter from Leonato to Friar Francis
- Dogberry's report.

Put your character's point of view. How might he or she feel about what is to take place tomorrow?

---

beliest thyself wrong yourself
bethink you of it think about it
Impose . . . penance make me
  suffer whatever punishment
enjoin commit

Possess inform
labour . . . invention produce
  anything by way of a poetic tribute
Give her the right i.e. make her
  your wife

Enter LEONATO, *his brother* [ANTONIO] *and the Sexton*

LEONATO Which is the villain? Let me see his eyes,
⠀⠀⠀⠀⠀⠀That when I note another man like him,
⠀⠀⠀⠀⠀⠀I may avoid him: which of these is he?
BORACHIO If you would know your wronger, look on me.
LEONATO Art thou the slave that with thy breath hast killed⠀⠀⠀⠀⠀230
⠀⠀⠀⠀⠀⠀Mine innocent child?
BORACHIO⠀⠀⠀⠀⠀⠀⠀⠀⠀⠀⠀⠀⠀Yea, even I alone.
LEONATO No, not so, villain, thou beliest thyself,
⠀⠀⠀⠀⠀⠀Here stand a pair of honourable men,
⠀⠀⠀⠀⠀⠀A third is fled that had a hand in it:
⠀⠀⠀⠀⠀⠀I thank you, princes, for my daughter's death,⠀⠀⠀⠀⠀235
⠀⠀⠀⠀⠀⠀Record it with your high and worthy deeds,
⠀⠀⠀⠀⠀⠀'Twas bravely done, if you bethink you of it.
CLAUDIO I know not how to pray your patience,
⠀⠀⠀⠀⠀⠀Yet I must speak, choose your revenge yourself,
⠀⠀⠀⠀⠀⠀Impose me to what penance your invention⠀⠀⠀⠀⠀240
⠀⠀⠀⠀⠀⠀Can lay upon my sin, yet sinned I not,
⠀⠀⠀⠀⠀⠀But in mistaking.
DON PEDRO⠀⠀⠀⠀⠀⠀⠀⠀⠀⠀⠀By my soul nor I,
⠀⠀⠀⠀⠀⠀And yet to satisfy this good old man,
⠀⠀⠀⠀⠀⠀I would bend under any heavy weight,
⠀⠀⠀⠀⠀⠀That he'll enjoin me to.⠀⠀⠀⠀⠀245
LEONATO I cannot bid you bid my daughter live,
⠀⠀⠀⠀⠀⠀That were impossible, but I pray you both,
⠀⠀⠀⠀⠀⠀Possess the people in Messina here,
⠀⠀⠀⠀⠀⠀How innocent she died, and if your love
⠀⠀⠀⠀⠀⠀Can labour aught in sad invention,⠀⠀⠀⠀⠀250
⠀⠀⠀⠀⠀⠀Hang her an epitaph upon her tomb,
⠀⠀⠀⠀⠀⠀And sing it to her bones, sing it tonight:
⠀⠀⠀⠀⠀⠀Tomorrow morning come you to my house,
⠀⠀⠀⠀⠀⠀And since you could not be my son-in-law,
⠀⠀⠀⠀⠀⠀Be yet my nephew: my brother hath a daughter,⠀⠀⠀⠀⠀255
⠀⠀⠀⠀⠀⠀Almost the copy of my child that's dead,
⠀⠀⠀⠀⠀⠀And she alone is heir to both of us,
⠀⠀⠀⠀⠀⠀Give her the right you should have given her cousin,
⠀⠀⠀⠀⠀⠀And so dies my revenge.
CLAUDIO⠀⠀⠀⠀⠀⠀⠀⠀⠀⠀⠀⠀Oh noble sir!
⠀⠀⠀⠀⠀⠀Your over kindness doth wring tears from me,⠀⠀⠀⠀⠀260

Borachio assures Leonato of Margaret's innocence in the whole affair.
Dogberry leaves, still very much concerned that no one should forget
that he has been called an ass.

1 Final thoughts on Dogberry (in groups of five or six)

Not even a prince, count and several signors can silence Dogberry!
This is the last we see of him. Do you like or despise him?

a Is Dogberry truly an ass?

Half the group gathers evidence to support this view. The other
half prepares his defence. Argue the case.

b How does Dogberry leave?

Act out your version of Dogberry's exit (lines 271–89). Look for
comic opportunities from the reactions of those present and from
the manner of Dogberry's leaving. Decide how hard he has to work
to get his money (line 282), and how much of it (if any) he gives to
Verges. One production made a very amusing use of the missed
handshake routine!

c 'The watch heard them talk of one Deformed'

In passing through the brain of Dogberry, the story of the notorious
villain Deformed has achieved an amazing degree of distortion.
It began in 3.3 where Borachio talked of 'that deformed thief
fashion'. The Watchman, mistaking what he heard for an actual
thief, declared that Deformed wore a lovelock (see page 172).

Dogberry is still doggedly pursuing this illusory villain, but what
has his brain done to the lovelock?

2 Imagine the scene (in pairs)

Improvise the scene in which Leonato asks Margaret to explain her
behaviour.

---

embrace seize upon
dispose . . . of from now on do
  what you like with
naughty wicked
packed involved
by her about her

under . . . black recorded in
  writing
foundation he gives thanks as if he
  had received alms at some religious
  institution
look for you will expect you
lewd base, worthless

> I do embrace your offer, and dispose
> For henceforth of poor Claudio.

LEONATO Tomorrow then I will expect your coming,
> Tonight I take my leave: this naughty man
> Shall face-to-face be brought to Margaret,   265
> Who I believe was packed in all this wrong,
> Hired to it by your brother.

BORACHIO   No by my soul she was not,
> Nor knew not what she did when she spoke to me,
> But always hath been just and virtuous
> In anything that I do know by her.   270

DOGBERRY Moreover, sir, which indeed is not under white and black, this plaintiff here, the offender, did call me ass, I beseech you let it be remembered in his punishment: and also the watch heard them talk of one Deformed, they say he wears a key in his ear, and a lock hanging by it, and borrows money in God's name, the which he hath 275 used so long, and never paid, that now men grow hard hearted and will lend nothing for God's sake: pray you examine him upon that point.

LEONATO I thank thee for thy care and honest pains.

DOGBERRY Your worship speaks like a most thankful and reverent 280 youth, and I praise God for you.

LEONATO There's for thy pains.

DOGBERRY God save the foundation.

LEONATO Go, I discharge thee of thy prisoner, and I thank thee.

DOGBERRY I leave an arrant knave with your worship, which I beseech 285 your worship to correct yourself, for the example of others: God keep your worship, I wish your worship well, God restore you to health, I humbly give you leave to depart, and if a merry meeting may be wished, God prohibit it: come, neighbour.

Exeunt [Dogberry and Verges]

LEONATO Until tomorrow morning, lords, farewell.   290

ANTONIO Farewell, my lords, we look for you tomorrow.

DON PEDRO We will not fail.

CLAUDIO   Tonight I'll mourn with Hero.

[Exeunt Don Pedro and Claudio]

LEONATO Bring you these fellows on, we'll talk with Margaret, how her acquaintance grew with this lewd fellow.

Exeunt

Benedick seeks Margaret's help in arranging a meeting with Beatrice. As he awaits Beatrice's arrival, he attempts a love song and laments his inability to express his love in rhyme.

1 More bawdy jokes (in groups of four)

Benedick and Margaret's remarks (lines 1–17) are full of *double entendres* (double meanings). Sexual innuendo runs through their conversation:

come over surpass (suggesting 'take sexually')
buckler shield (suggesting 'belly, vagina')
swords/pikes weapons (suggesting 'penis')
vice clamp (suggesting 'gripping thighs'?).

Either choose a reading using echo to emphasise the dirty jokes;
  or two of you read the dialogue while the other two make gestures and comments to highlight the sexual innuendoes;
  or prepare director's notes on the mood you want to create at the beginning of this scene and how you would create it;
  or debate whether all this is an early form of sexual harassment.

2 Benedick – soldier but no poet! (in small groups)

The ideal Elizabethan man was both soldier and poet. Songs, sonnets and blank verse were traditional ways for a lover to express his love. Benedick demonstrates his lack of skill in lines 18–22.

Write Benedick's pitiful attempt at a love poem for Beatrice. Incorporate the legendary lovers, Hero and Leander, and Troilus and Cressida (see pages 104 and 182). Use the rhymes Benedick mentions.

deserve . . . hands earn my gratitude
helping . . . speech getting me a chance to talk to
comely fitting
keep . . . stairs remain a servant
I give . . . bucklers I surrender

panders go-betweens
quondam former
carpet-mongers frequenters of ladies' bedrooms
in festival terms in the style of public display (i.e. speaking poetry)

ACT 5 SCENE 2
Leonato's garden

Enter BENEDICK *and* MARGARET

BENEDICK Pray thee, sweet Mistress Margaret, deserve well at my
hands, by helping me to the speech of Beatrice.

MARGARET Will you then write me a sonnet in praise of my beauty?

BENEDICK In so high a style, Margaret, that no man living shall come
over it, for in most comely truth thou deservest it.   5

MARGARET To have no man come over me, why, shall I always keep
below stairs?

BENEDICK Thy wit is as quick as the greyhound's mouth, it catches.

MARGARET And yours, as blunt as the fencers' foils, which hit, but hurt
not.   10

BENEDICK A most manly wit, Margaret, it will not hurt a woman: and so
I pray thee call Beatrice, I give thee the bucklers.

MARGARET Give us the swords, we have bucklers of our own.

BENEDICK If you use them, Margaret, you must put in the pikes with a
vice, and they are dangerous weapons for maids.   15

MARGARET Well, I will call Beatrice to you, who I think hath legs. *Exit*

BENEDICK And therefore will come.

[*Sings*]   The God of love
                   That sits above,
                   And knows me,   20
                   And knows me:
                   How pitiful I deserve.

I mean in singing, but in loving – Leander the good swimmer,
Troilus, the first employer of panders, and a whole book full of
these quondam carpet-mongers, whose names yet run smoothly in   25
the even road of a blank verse, why they were never so truly turned
over and over as my poor self in love: marry, I cannot show it in
rhyme, I have tried: I can find out no rhyme to lady but baby, an
innocent rhyme: for scorn horn, a hard rhyme: for school fool, a
babbling rhyme: very ominous endings. No, I was not born under a   30
rhyming planet, nor I cannot woo in festival terms.

Benedick tells Beatrice that he has challenged Claudio and then asks her how she first fell in love with him. She in turn asks Benedick how he first fell in love with her.

1 Swords, shields or truth (in groups of four)

Even when they are courting, Benedick and Beatrice cannot stop arguing. 'Thou and I are too wise to woo peaceably', he remarks in line 54.

Decide how frank they are with each other. Two of you sit face to face and slowly read lines 32–79. The other two sit beside each character and arm themselves with a sword (rolled-up sheet of paper) and a shield (book).

As Beatrice and Benedick speak to each other they must prod with the sword if they think their character is attacking, raise the shield if they are on the defensive and put both down if they are being truly open and honest. Change roles and try it again.

Compare the way Beatrice and Benedick talk to each other here with the way in which they talked to each other in 1.1 and 2.1. It is also interesting to compare their way of courting with Hero and Claudio's (especially 2.1.225–40).

2 Thou and you again

Which form does Benedick use to address Beatrice and which form does she use towards him? Can you explain the difference? Keep a note of how they address each other from now on.

---

that I came what I came for (i.e. to know about the challenge)
noisome disgusting, smelly
undergoes accepts
subscribe him write him down as
so politic a state such a well-organised rule

suffer (1) experience (2) put up with
spite it trouble it
there's not . . . himself self-praise is no recommendation
instance saying, proverb
that . . . neighbours untrue now

Enter BEATRICE

Sweet Beatrice, wouldst thou come when I called thee?

BEATRICE Yea, signor, and depart when you bid me.

BENEDICK Oh stay but till then.

BEATRICE Then, is spoken: fare you well now, and yet ere I go, let me   35
go with that I came, which is, with knowing what hath passed
between you and Claudio.

BENEDICK Only foul words, and thereupon I will kiss thee.

BEATRICE Foul words is but foul wind, and foul wind is but foul breath,
and foul breath is noisome, therefore I will depart unkissed.   40

BENEDICK Thou hast frighted the word out of his right sense, so forc-
ible is thy wit: but I must tell thee plainly, Claudio undergoes my
challenge, and either I must shortly hear from him, or I will subscribe him a coward: and I pray thee now tell me, for which of my
bad parts didst thou first fall in love with me?   45

BEATRICE For them all together, which maintained so politic a state of
evil, that they will not admit any good part to intermingle with them:
but for which of my good parts did you first suffer love for me?

BENEDICK Suffer love! A good epithet: I do suffer love indeed, for I
love thee against my will.   50

BEATRICE In spite of your heart I think: alas poor heart, if you spite it
for my sake, I will spite it for yours, for I will never love that which
my friend hates.

BENEDICK Thou and I are too wise to woo peaceably.

BEATRICE It appears not in this confession, there's not one wise man   55
among twenty that will praise himself.

BENEDICK An old, an old instance, Beatrice, that lived in the time of
good neighbours: if a man do not erect in this age his own tomb ere
he dies, he shall live no longer in monument than the bell rings and
the widow weeps.   60

*As Benedick and Beatrice talk, Ursula comes rushing in with news that
Don John's plot has been discovered. All three leave in haste for
Leonato's house.*

'Coming to a mutual likeness.'

1 Beatrice and Benedick

Look back at the pictures of Beatrice and Benedick (pages 32, 118,
126) and talk about their changing moods and attitudes. How would
you describe their relationship in this scene?

Question Good question!
clamour noise (of the funeral bell)
rheum weeping (of the widow)
Don Worm in the Bible,
conscience is a tormenting worm
eating a man's spirit

mend get better
yonder's old coil there's an awful
commotion
abused deceived, imposed upon
die in thy lap sexual innuendo

BEATRICE And how long is that think you?

BENEDICK Question: why an hour in clamour and a quarter in rheum, therefore is it most expedient for the wise, if Don Worm (his conscience) find no impediment to the contrary, to be the trumpet of his own virtues, as I am to myself; so much for praising myself, who I   65
myself will bear witness is praiseworthy: and now tell me, how doth your cousin?

BEATRICE Very ill.

BENEDICK And how do you?

BEATRICE Very ill too.   70

BENEDICK Serve God, love me, and mend: there will I leave you too, for here comes one in haste.

Enter URSULA

URSULA Madam, you must come to your uncle, yonder's old coil at home, it is proved my Lady Hero hath been falsely accused, the prince and Claudio mightily abused, and Don John is the author of   75
all, who is fled and gone: will you come presently?

BEATRICE Will you go hear this news, signor?

BENEDICK I will live in thy heart, die in thy lap, and be buried in thy eyes: and moreover, I will go with thee to thy uncle's.

Exeunt

Night. In a sombre ceremony, Claudio fulfils the first part of his promise.
A tribute to Hero is read out, a solemn hymn is sung and a vow made
to commemorate the anniversary of her death.

1 A grim reminder (in groups of about seven)

In Act 4 the play moved from light into dark. Now it moves back from darkness into light, both literally (lines 24–8) and symbolically. In one production, the lights dimmed, a tomb-like monument rose up from beneath the stage, and shadowy figures entered bearing flickering torches.

Create your own dramatically effective scene of solemn ritual. Consider:

- using choral speaking and echo effects
- highlighting the sound patterns of the rhymed verse
- the stage direction 'Enter . . . with tapers and music'
- what line 30 suggests about the costumes.

2 Who says what? (in small groups)

No one can be quite sure about who Shakespeare intended to speak lines 3–23. One production had:

- Claudio reading out the epitaph (lines 3–10) and speaking lines 22–3
- Balthasar singing the song (lines 12–21).

How would you allocate the lines? Give reasons for your choices.

3 Did Claudio write the epitaph? (in groups of three)

Find the line in 5.1 where Leonato instructs Claudio to compose an epitaph to hang on Hero's tomb. Read the actual epitaph (lines 3–10) and debate whether it sounds like the sort of thing Claudio would write.

---

tapers lights
monument tomb, burial chamber
guerdon of recompense for
goddess of the night Diana, moon
  goddess and patroness of virgins

virgin knight devout servant
  (Hero, a virgin, is imagined as a
  follower of Diana)
rite ceremony

ACT 5   SCENE 3
Hero's monument

Enter CLAUDIO, DON PEDRO *and three or four Attendants with tapers and music*

CLAUDIO Is this the monument of Leonato?

LORD It is, my lord.

[He reads the] epitaph

> Done to death by slanderous tongues,
> Was the Hero that here lies:
> Death in guerdon of her wrongs,   5
> Gives her fame which never dies:
> So the life that died with shame,
> Lives in death with glorious fame.
> Hang thou there upon the tomb,
> Praising her when I am dumb.   10

CLAUDIO Now music sound and sing your solemn hymn.

Song

> Pardon, goddess of the night,
> Those that slew thy virgin knight,
> For the which with songs of woe,
> Round about her tomb they go: 15
> Midnight assist our moan,
> Help us to sigh and groan.
> Heavily, heavily.
> Graves yawn and yield your dead,
> Till death be utterèd,   20
> Heavily, heavily.

LORD
> Now unto thy bones good night,
> Yearly will I do this rite.

As dawn breaks, Don Pedro and Claudio leave to dress suitably for the marriage. Scene 4 opens with Leonato sending the women to mask themselves in readiness for the ceremony.

A modern setting of the monument scene.

1 Who's who?

Looking at the picture above, identify Claudio, Don Pedro, the unnamed lord, the musicians and singers, the attendants with tapers.

2 Night ends and a new day begins

What kind of dawn seems to be breaking at the end of Scene 3, and what kind of night has it been?

We are now at the final scene. Do you think it will all end happily? Quickly read through Scene 4. Are there any surprises?

Phoebus Apollo, the sun god, who drives his chariot across the sky
several separate
weeds clothes (what does this change of clothes symbolise?)
Hymen god of marriage

issue outcome
Than this Hero's death
against her will unintentionally
question investigation
sorts have turned out
confirmed countenance a straight face

DON PEDRO Good morrow, masters, put your torches out,
　　　　The wolves have preyed, and look, the gentle day　　　25
　　　　Before the wheels of Phoebus, round about
　　　　Dapples the drowsy east with spots of grey:
　　　　Thanks to you all, and leave us, fare you well.
CLAUDIO Good morrow, masters, each his several way.

[Exeunt Attendants]

DON PEDRO Come let us hence, and put on other weeds,　　　30
　　　　And then to Leonato's we will go.
CLAUDIO And Hymen now with luckier issue speeds,
　　　　Than this for whom we rendered up this woe.

Exeunt

ACT 5　SCENE 4
Leonato's house

Enter LEONATO, BENEDICK, MARGARET, URSULA, ANTONIO,
FRIAR FRANCIS and HERO

FRIAR FRANCIS Did I not tell you she was innocent?
LEONATO So are the prince and Claudio who accused her,
　　　　Upon the error that you heard debated:
　　　　But Margaret was in some fault for this,
　　　　Although against her will as it appears,　　　5
　　　　In the true course of all the question.
ANTONIO Well, I am glad that all things sorts so well.
BENEDICK And so am I, being else by faith enforced
　　　　To call young Claudio to a reckoning for it.
LEONATO Well, daughter, and you gentlewomen all,　　　10
　　　　Withdraw into a chamber by yourselves,
　　　　And when I send for you come hither masked:
　　　　The prince and Claudio promised by this hour
　　　　To visit me: you know your office, brother,
　　　　You must be father to your brother's daughter,　　　15
　　　　And give her to young Claudio.

Exeunt Ladies

ANTONIO Which I will do with confirmed countenance.

Benedick requests Beatrice's hand in marriage, to which Leonato willingly agrees. Claudio and Don Pedro arrive for the wedding ceremony and continue their mockery of Benedick.

1 'Your answer, sir, is enigmatical' (in pairs)

Benedick formally asks permission to marry Beatrice (lines 21–31) and seems confused by Leonato's 'enigmatical' (puzzling) responses. Read lines 21–31 to each other. Do you think Benedick is still unaware of the trick played on him?

2 Good friends once again? (in groups of three)

When Benedick, Claudio and Don Pedro last met (5.1.109–84), relations between them were strained. Benedick challenged Claudio and there was considerable hostility.

Improvise. Take a part each and speak your thoughts in role as you meet your former friends. Make clear your feelings about your last meeting. Benedick should account for his 'February face'.

Now sit face to face and read lines 40–52 (up to '. . . For this I owe you'). Is your mockery friendly or aggressive? Are you all friends again? The 'thou/you' pronouns may give you some ideas (see page 165).

3 Divine cuckolding

Jupiter (Jove), the father of the gods, took on the form of a bull in order to carry off Europa, the beautiful daughter of a Phoenician king (see page 182). Europa also means Europe.

Which of Benedick's comments from Act 1 Scene 1 is Claudio hinting at in lines 43–7? Explain the insult that Benedick gives in reply.

---

intreat . . . pains beg to trouble you
undo ruin
requite her return her love
will desire
hold my mind keep to my intention

Ethiop black (pale skin was a mark of beauty to the Elizabethans – see page 183)
tip thy horns with gold make you look a fine cuckold
low bellow
got fathered

BENEDICK Friar, I must intreat your pains, I think.

FRIAR FRANCIS To do what, signor?

BENEDICK To bind me, or undo me, one of them: 20
  Signor Leonato, truth it is, good signor,
  Your niece regards me with an eye of favour.

LEONATO That eye my daughter lent her, 'tis most true.

BENEDICK And I do with an eye of love requite her.

LEONATO The sight whereof I think you had from me, 25
  From Claudio and the prince, but what's your will?

BENEDICK Your answer, sir, is enigmatical,
  But for my will, my will is, your good will
  May stand with ours, this day to be conjoined,
  In the state of honourable marriage,   30
  In which (good friar) I shall desire your help.

LEONATO My heart is with your liking.

FRIAR FRANCIS   And my help.
  Here comes the prince and Claudio.

Enter DON PEDRO *and* CLAUDIO, *with Attendants*

DON PEDRO Good morrow to this fair assembly.

LEONATO Good morrow, prince, good morrow, Claudio: 35
  We here attend you, are you yet determined,
  Today to marry with my brother's daughter?

CLAUDIO I'll hold my mind were she an Ethiop.

LEONATO Call her forth, brother, here's the friar ready.

            [*Exit Antonio*]

DON PEDRO Good morrow, Benedick, why what's the matter, 40
  That you have such a February face,
  So full of frost, of storm, and cloudiness?

CLAUDIO I think he thinks upon the savage bull:
  Tush fear not, man, we'll tip thy horns with gold,
  And all Europa shall rejoice at thee,   45
  As once Europa did at lusty Jove,
  When he would play the noble beast in love.

BENEDICK Bull Jove, sir, had an amiable low,
  And some such strange bull leaped your father's cow,
  And got a calf in that same noble feat,   50
  Much like to you, for you have just his bleat.

Antonio brings in four masked ladies. Claudio accepts his unknown bride and discovers she is Hero. Beatrice and Benedick realise they have been tricked into believing that each was in love with the other.

1 Masks off (in groups of seven)

This is a serious and tense moment for Claudio and Hero. Claudio has no idea who is to be his bride and Hero will be awaiting his reaction when she unmasks. Beatrice and Benedick, for their part, will be required to remove their psychological masks and publicly admit their love. Choose from the following:

a Act out lines 52–71. Make this second betrothal a solemn and moving occasion. Use masks or veils, and think about the timing of the actual moment of unmasking. At the end of your dramatisation, Claudio and Hero should speak in role explaining their actions.

b Shakespeare often uses this unmasking device. In *Twelfth Night*, Viola's real identity is revealed when her male disguise is removed. In *The Winter's Tale* a 'dead' wife is found to be alive (she too had been wronged and kept hidden just as Hero has been). Talk together about the meaning of this strange unmasking ceremony. Why must there be a 'new' Hero? Do we also have a 'new' Claudio?

c 'No more than reason' (lines 74 and 77). Rehearse different ways of saying these lines. What do you think Beatrice and Benedick mean?

d Rehearse your version of lines 72–96. After the solemnity of Claudio and Hero's betrothal, make this event more light-hearted. Many productions look to get laughs from the business with the sonnets, and again with the kiss at line 96.

For this I owe you I'll pay you back for this
reckonings obligations
defiled slandered
but whiles only so long as
qualify moderate

largely in full, in detail
let wonder seem familiar treat your amazement as an everyday event
Soft and fair wait a minute
but in . . . recompense only as a friend

Enter ANTONIO, HERO, BEATRICE, MARGARET [*and*]
URSULA [*masked*]

CLAUDIO For this I owe you: here comes other reckonings.
    Which is the lady I must seize upon?
LEONATO This same is she, and I do give you her.
CLAUDIO Why then she's mine, sweet, let me see your face.   55
LEONATO No that you shall not, till you take her hand,
    Before this friar, and swear to marry her.
CLAUDIO Give me your hand before this holy friar,
    I am your husband if you like of me.
HERO And when I lived I was your other wife,   60
    And when you loved, you were my other husband.
CLAUDIO Another Hero?
HERO   Nothing certainer.
    One Hero died defiled, but I do live,
    And surely as I live, I am a maid.
DON PEDRO The former Hero, Hero that is dead.   65
LEONATO She died, my lord, but whiles her slander lived.
FRIAR FRANCIS All this amazement can I qualify,
    When after that the holy rites are ended,
    I'll tell you largely of fair Hero's death:
    Meantime let wonder seem familiar,   70
    And to the chapel let us presently.
BENEDICK Soft and fair friar, which is Beatrice?
BEATRICE I answer to that name, what is your will?
BENEDICK Do not you love me?
BEATRICE   Why no, no more than reason.
BENEDICK Why then your uncle, and the prince, and Claudio,   75
    Have been deceived, they swore you did.
BEATRICE Do not you love me?
BENEDICK   Troth no, no more than reason.
BEATRICE Why then my cousin, Margaret and Ursula
    Are much deceived, for they did swear you did.
BENEDICK They swore that you were almost sick for me.   80
BEATRICE They swore that you were wellnigh dead for me.
BENEDICK 'Tis no such matter, then you do not love me?
BEATRICE No truly, but in friendly recompense.
LEONATO Come, cousin, I am sure you love the gentleman.
CLAUDIO And I'll be sworn upon't, that he loves her,   85

After being confronted with the love sonnets they have both written, Beatrice and Benedick agree to accept each other. Benedick and Claudio are reconciled. News comes of Don John's capture. The dancing begins.

1 Ending the play (in small groups)

It is the convention in a comedy that all differences are eventually resolved. But how happy should the play's final moments be? Explore your views on the play's ending by choosing one or more of the following:

a Benedick dominates the final moments of the play, but why is Beatrice so uncharacteristically silent? Write her thoughts.

b Act out a version of lines 104–12 in which Hero and Beatrice play a part in reconciling Claudio and Benedick. Then try a more hostile final encounter between the two men.

c Talk together about the kind of music and dancing that would most fittingly end the play. Think back to the masked dance in 2.1 and decide how different you would want the final dance to be.

d Don Pedro is often left to stand alone at the end of the play. What are his thoughts as he watches the dancers?

e Devise the closing image (the last thing the audience sees as the lights dim) for a production by each of the following: a feminist director (the woman's point of view), a Marxist director (money and power are dominant), a Freudian director (unconscious desires dominate). Then devise the closing image for your own production.

f Organise the curtain call and decide on a typical gesture/action for each character. Who enters and leaves with whom?

---

witcrackers jokers
flout mock
care for am hurt by
make . . . dealer make you take a
partner (but 'double dealer' also
meant 'deceiver', or 'unfaithful
husband')

do not . . . narrowly to thee does
not keep a very close eye on you
staff . . . horn staff of office or
walking stick (with cuckolding hints
of course)
ta'en captured

For here's a paper written in his hand,
A halting sonnet of his own pure brain,
Fashioned to Beatrice.

HERO   And here's another,
Writ in my cousin's hand, stol'n from her pocket,
Containing her affection unto Benedick.   90

BENEDICK A miracle, here's our own hands against our hearts: come, I
will have thee, but by this light I take thee for pity.

BEATRICE I would not deny you, but by this good day, I yield upon great
persuasion, and partly to save your life, for I was told, you were in a
consumption.   95

BENEDICK Peace I will stop your mouth.

DON PEDRO How dost thou, Benedick the married man?

BENEDICK I'll tell thee what, prince: a college of witcrackers cannot
flout me out of my humour: dost thou think I care for a satire or an
epigram? No, if a man will be beaten with brains, a shall wear   100
nothing handsome about him: in brief, since I do purpose to marry,
I will think nothing to any purpose that the world can say against it,
and therefore never flout at me, for what I have said against it: for
man is a giddy thing, and this is my conclusion: for thy part,
Claudio, I did think to have beaten thee, but in that thou art like to 105
be my kinsman, live unbruised, and love my cousin.

CLAUDIO I had well hoped thou wouldst have denied Beatrice, that I
might have cudgelled thee out of thy single life, to make thee a
double dealer, which out of question thou wilt be, if my cousin do
not look exceeding narrowly to thee.   110

BENEDICK Come, come, we are friends, let's have a dance ere we are
married, that we may lighten our own hearts, and our wives' heels.

LEONATO We'll have dancing afterward.

BENEDICK First, of my word, therefore play music. Prince, thou art sad,
get thee a wife, get thee a wife, there is no staff more reverend than   115
one tipped with horn.

Enter MESSENGER

MESSENGER My lord, your brother John is ta'en in flight,
And brought with armed men back to Messina.

BENEDICK Think not on him till tomorrow, I'll devise thee brave
punishments for him: strike up, pipers.   120
Dance [and exeunt]

Looking back at the play

Mini-saga

A 'mini-saga challenge' requires you to tell a story in exactly fifty words. Write the events of Act 5 as a mini-saga. Read your version and listen to other people's mini-sagas. What are the key events that you have all included?

Moods

Act 5 contains many changes of mood: grief, despair, anger, vengeance, repentance, love, mockery, celebration. Prepare director's notes for Act 5. Indicate when and where you want to create a change of mood (on which entrances and which lines).

Then act out your 'Mood change show'. You might call out the mood and have a character deliver the relevant lines in an appropriate tone. You could use mime, or a combination of words, actions and pictures.

Borachio's nightmare

Borachio's conscience is troubled by the part he has played in Hero's life. Invent a short play called 'Borachio's Nightmare' in which all Borachio's past actions come back to haunt him. If you wish, he can be woken up by Margaret, or would she too be part of the haunting?

Claudio – a postscript to his epitaph

At the beginning of Act 5 Scene 3, Claudio's eight-line epitaph to Hero was recited. It was a public tribute and a formal expression of grief.

Write Claudio's private postscript to that epitaph. This account should tell the real story, and make Claudio's true feelings very clear. Use a style of prose similar to the way in which he speaks in the play.

Swords and gloves

The sword and fencing glove used by the Beatrice pictured on page 2 made several appearances in that production of the play. Decide where the following incidents might have occurred:

- The sword used by Beatrice in the opening fight is later flexed behind her as she looks at Benedick.
- Beatrice's fencing glove is thrown down in a challenge to Benedick. The glove is picked up and the challenge accepted.
- Benedick takes out Beatrice's fencing glove and looks at it as if it were a love token.
- Benedick pauses and touches Beatrice's glove kept in his belt before throwing down his own gauntlet in challenge.

Cliffhangers

Imagine that the story of *Much Ado About Nothing* is to be dramatised in a new six-part television series. Divide the play into six parts and perform the last minute of each episode. Remember that you must end episodes one to five on a note of suspense so that your audience will watch the following week.

After the dance

At the end of Act 5, Beatrice and Benedick steal away from the dance to talk. Improvise their conversation as they look back over their strange courtship. You could have other students in role as Beatrice and Benedick, miming the events in your improvised dialogue.

Happy couples?

The play ends on an apparently happy note, with most differences resolved. The sincerity of both young men has been tested. Benedick agreed to fight for Beatrice's sake and the penitent Claudio submitted to Leonato's wishes. But will their marriages be successful?

It is five years later. The two couples are visitors at Leonato's house. Which of the two couples is more secure and happy? Are Benedick and Claudio fully reconciled? To explore these issues choose one of the following:

- improvise this reunion scene or write a script for it
- improvise what happens when the two couples go to see a marriage guidance counsellor
- interview the couples as a reporter for a popular weekly magazine.

What is the play about?

Much ado about many things

Much Ado About Nothing has always been a popular play. A verse published in 1640 showed how it filled theatres:

'Let but Beatrice
And Benedick be seen, lo in a trice
The Cockpit, galleries, boxes, all are full.'

The appeal of the 'merry war' has a lot to do with the play's lasting popularity, but there are many more reasons. Its themes have universal appeal: love, status, relationships between men and women, the ways in which we perceive one another. The moods of the play swing from light comedy to dark, life-endangering menace. There is always something happening: a fresh break-out of an old conflict, another plot, another mistaking, even songs and dancing!

- List the themes you think Shakespeare is exploring in the play. Which ones are still relevant today?
- A modern English version of *Much Ado About Nothing* is about to go on peak time popular television. Prepare and present a two minute trailer for this programme which gives the audience ten reasons for watching.

Two pairs of lovers

The Beatrice/Benedick story seems to be Shakespeare's own invention, but the Hero/Claudio narrative has a long history. The tale of how a lover is deceived into believing that his beloved has been unfaithful to him because he has seen a man at her bedroom window goes back many centuries. Shakespeare probably based his Hero/Claudio story on Italian versions popular in Elizabethan England.

- Talk together about why you think Shakespeare pairs a 'modern' love story and 'traditional' one.
- Can you identify incidents in contemporary plays and television programmes which draw on the Hero/Claudio story?

Reflecting society and everyday life

Despite the foreign names, Messina is a very English community, not unlike the household of a wealthy Elizabethan lord. Many Elizabethan sports and pastimes are mentioned in the play: angling, archery, falconry, eating and drinking, gambling, brothel-haunting, fighting.

- Brainstorm! In a three-minute session, jot down your impressions of the society Shakespeare shows us.
- Assign each scene in the play to a particular place and time of day. Include in your time/place pattern all the domestic events and ceremonies that take place in this community (meals, weddings, funerals).

Male power, status and honour

In Shakespeare's plays the pronouns 'Thou/thee/thine' and 'You/your' send clear social signals. When addressing one person, the use of 'You' implies distance, suggesting respect for your superior, or courtesy to your social equal. 'Thou' can imply either closeness or superiority. It can signal friendship towards an equal or superiority over a servant. Used to address one of higher rank, it can be aggressive and insulting.

- Rank, respect, allegiance and friendship are put to the test when Claudio denounces Hero. Identify how Benedick and Leonato use the 'thou/you' forms in Act 5 to address Claudio.
- Explore how Benedick's growing love for Beatrice changes the way he addresses her in Acts 4 and 5. Can you explain why Beatrice still keeps to the 'you' form to address him, even in the final scenes?
- Explain why Dogberry uses both 'thou' and 'you' to address Borachio and Conrade in 4.2.
- The people of rank in the play are all men. Don Pedro is a prince, his brother and Claudio are counts (equivalent to an English earl). 'Signors' Benedick and Leonato are gentlemen of lower rank.
- When these five men speak to each other in Act 1, do they behave strictly according to their rank?
- Don Pedro and Claudio are described as having 'the very bent of honour' (4.1.179). Do you agree?

The threat of an outsider

Secure and undisputed inheritance of property was very important to the Elizabethan aristocracy. Since he was born out of wedlock, a bastard threatened to challenge the claims of the legitimate heirs. Elizabethans therefore regarded a bastard as evil and malicious.

How much of a threat is Don John to his brother and to Messina society?

The Watch

Dogberry, Verges and the Watch are Shakespeare's own invention but were probably modelled on real-life characters (see page 78). They give us a brief glimpse of the Elizabethan lower classes and provide much amusement (the part of Dogberry was originally written for Will Kemp, the resident clown of Shakespeare's company of actors). However, the Watch also provide a commentary on the gentry whom they serve and 'protect'.

- How are Dogberry and the Watch (a) different from their aristocratic superiors (b) similar to them?
- Give reasons to support the idea that Dogberry is the real hero of the play.

Tangled webs (in small groups)

The play has three major dramatic plots or stories (the Hero/Claudio love story, the tricking into love of Beatrice and Benedick, the Don John plot which is discovered by Dogberry). The close-knit nature of Messina society, where everybody wants to know everybody else's business, is reflected in the way in which these three plots are so closely interwoven. On a large piece of paper, make three columns for the three plots and write the scenes in order down the left-hand side. On this grid briefly record, scene by scene, each stage in the development of each plot and the names of the characters involved in the action. Work as a group to share the load.

- Which characters are most entangled in the events of all three plots?
- Which characters are the catalysts or the initiators of events?
- The Beatrice and Benedick story was traditionally regarded as a sub-plot, and the Hero/Claudio story seen as the main plot. Can you explain why?

Tricks, hoaxes and deceptions

The play contains many tricks and deceptions, both deliberate and accidental.

- Malevolent and benevolent plots, deliberate and accidental deceptions. Compile your own collection of each.
- One writer said that the play 'is composed of three hoaxes, four with-held secrets and three metamorphoses'. What do you think these might be?

Nothing and noting, truth and illusion

The punning on 'nothing' and 'noting' in the title (see pages 10 and 50) suggests from the start that the play will be concerned with ways in which people perceive one another. Characters are continually faced with the question: 'Can I be certain that what I see, or hear, or know is true?' Their difficulties are often caused by the deliberate deceptions of others, but equally often stem from self-deception or their own human fallibility.

Make a list of the problems facing characters in the play under these three headings: deliberate deception, self-deception, and human fallibility. Do you think the play gives any answers to the problem that we all face: 'How can I ever know the truth for certain?'

The Truth and Illusion Theatre Company have come to Messina to present a show which will reveal all the deceptions and self-deceptions that have taken place during the past few days. Be as inventive as you can in finding ways of highlighting the many comic and serious deceptions.

'Men were deceivers ever'

Kenneth Branagh's 1993 film of *Much Ado About Nothing* begins with Beatrice ironically speaking the song (from Act 2 Scene 3) 'Sigh no more, ladies, sigh no more'. Turn to page 53 to remind yourself of the song. Then talk together about how much you think it catches the spirit of the whole play.

Beatrice and Benedick

An actor's thoughts on Beatrice and Benedick

Actors must 'find' their character as the play comes to life around them in rehearsal and performance. Susan Fleetwood (pictured on pages 118 and 150) talks below about what she 'found' when she played Beatrice.

Two lonely people?

'Beatrice is life-giving, energetic, witty, intelligent, fun-loving, but lonely. In playing her, I was conscious of her as the orphaned cousin, being on the outside of things in many ways. Yet her position in the household also allows her freedom to be outrageous in a way that Hero cannot be.'

Collect evidence from the play to back up this description of Beatrice. What reasons, besides being the 'orphaned cousin', can you give for thinking she is lonely? Or is 'loner' a better word?

Do you think Benedick is also lonely?

Two individualists?

'Beatrice has an absolute hatred of the hypocrisy of the age, of all the sham nonsense and social hierarchy which aims to control. She has no patience with all the military hyperbole and bravado and is also detached from all the courtly ceremony and ritual. That's why I stood apart from the group, waiting, observing, flexing the sword I'd just used in the mock fight with Leonato.'

Work in pairs. One of you is Beatrice the conformist, the other Beatrice the rebel. Together, recount the events of the play, each one speaking at appropriate moments.

At what points in the play is Benedick also prepared to stand by what he believes?

Beatrice the critic of masculine values

'She doesn't only challenge the accepted opinion of war, she is critical of all masculine values. She is a mature woman who rages against the masculine solidarity which can so easily destroy a woman's reputation. She means it when she says "Kill Claudio".'

Find six occasions where Beatrice speaks critically of male behaviour. Speak the lines to each other as scornfully as you can.

How important is Benedick to Beatrice?

'The choice that Benedick makes when Beatrice asks him to kill Claudio is critical to her entire future. Had he chosen otherwise, Beatrice might have been doomed to a future as an isolated, shrewish woman and Benedick to a future as a drunken roué (debaucher). Beatrice needs to be played passionately here, for underlying her jokes and anger is a vulnerable awareness that she could lose everything.'

Work in pairs as Beatrice and Benedick. It is your tenth wedding anniversary and you are reminiscing. Tell each other why the moment when Beatrice said 'Kill Claudio' was so important to you and how different life would have been if Benedick had chosen differently.

A tried and tested relationship?

'By the end of the play Beatrice and Benedick have gained in self-knowledge and earned each other, in contrast to Claudio and Hero who have undergone a crash course in relationships.'

Talk about what self-knowledge you think Beatrice and Benedick have gained by the end of the play. What does 'a crash course in relationships' suggest is wrong with Claudio and Hero's courtship?

Beatrice and Benedick's final kiss and dance

'At the end of the play Beatrice is a liberated character who flings herself into the dance in celebration. The kiss is a real physical commitment, indicative of her love and passion. Unless the audience really believes that Beatrice and Benedick want to be together, there is no real joy at the end.'

If you were playing Benedick, would that be your view of the ending?

What is your picture of Beatrice?

Sinead Cusack's portrayal of Beatrice (see pages 32 and 126) was rather different from Susan Fleetwood's. In the opening scenes she was a bouncy, self-confident and flirtatious young woman who made the audience far more sympathetic towards the discomforted Bene-dick, until his flight from 'this Harpy' brought her to the edge of tears and exposed her vulnerability.

A more 'violent' Beatrice in the 1979 RSC production.

Talk together about the qualities you would want to see brought out in your ideal portrayal of Beatrice. Do you agree with any of the views expressed so far? Look back over pages 168–9 and identify the views with which you disagree. Give reasons for your disagreement.

Prepare the role of Benedick

Imagine that you are preparing to act the part of Benedick. You could:

- Make notes on how you think he should be played in each scene in which he appears. Decide how you think he develops during the play.
- Record details of any changes of costume and make-up needed.
- Collect examples of his language.
- Make a list of what he actually does throughout the play – actions reveal character.
- Explore his motives by 'hot seating' him. One person takes on the role. Others question or probe his motives and actions in the play.

An actor's view of Benedick

'*Much Ado About Nothing* is a physical endurance test. It's full of song and dance and I never seem to stop. I'm absolutely exhausted.'

Derek Jacobi (the Benedick pictured on pages 32 and 126)

Talk about the ways in which an actor could create an all-action Benedick.

Would it be possible to play a 'relaxed' Benedick? If you think it is, give examples of how to play certain parts of the script.

How would you cast Beatrice and Benedick?

If you were casting the two roles, which qualities would you look for in the actors? Think especially about how your two choices would complement each other. Susan Fleetwood would not accept the role of Beatrice until she knew who was to play the part of Benedick. The 1993 film of the play starred Kenneth Branagh and Emma Thompson in the roles of Beatrice and Benedick. In real life they are husband and wife. Which actors or public personalities do you think would make suitable pairings? Suggest some unsuitable pairings, and say why they are unsuitable.

Developing the roles of Beatrice and Benedick in rehearsal

One company in rehearsal developed their idea of Beatrice and Benedick by talking about what might have happened between them before the play began.

Create your 'history' of Beatrice and Benedick which explains their behaviour in 1.1 and 2.1. Find clues in the script to justify your invention.

The play has just begun. In pairs, speak for a minute in role, one as Beatrice, the other as Benedick. Talk about the past and how you feel about meeting each other again. What differences do you notice?

Women in a patriarchal world

Men (particularly fathers) dominated Elizabethan society. The play explores a wide range of men's attitudes to the place of women in society.

'Oh Lord! The queen is a woman!' exclaimed one woman when she saw Queen Elizabeth I passing in procession. Such traditional assumptions of male superiority were widespread. A wife should submit to her husband. She was his legal property and rarely expected to think for herself.

'England is a paradise for women', said one foreign visitor to London. Women in the capital certainly enjoyed a degree of freedom. Queen Elizabeth I showed that a woman could match any man. She was highly educated, fluent in several languages and a skilful politician.

Elizabethan men drew on a variety of stereotyped views about women as they attempted to explain, justify and control the place of woman in society:

a **Woman as whore or wife**   Women had just two functions. They were either prostitutes to be bought or wives to be owned.

b **Woman as goddess**   The courtly lover placed woman on a pedestal to be worshipped. Such idolatry could submerge the individual: 'To see a woman as a goddess is to silence her as a human being'.

c **Woman as adulterer**   Virginity was a virtue and adultery an unforgivable sin. The fear of a bastard intruding on the succession of property demanded that a bride should be a virgin and a wife should be faithful. An heiress who was proved unchaste was deprived of her inheritance.

d **Woman as shrew and scapegoat**   Women were a favourite target for satirists, who blamed them for the faults of the world. Any woman who attempted to speak up for herself was branded a shrew and needed taming!

What do the men in the play think?

Using the information opposite, find comments made by the men in the play which echo these attitudes. Do the women express similar sentiments?

Explain the profusion of jokes about cuckolds, curst cows, bulls, marriage and old maids.

Explain the venom of Claudio and Don Pedro's anger at Hero's 'disloyalty'.

What happened to all the mothers?

Beatrice is an orphan. Margaret and Ursula make no mention of their parents. Early copies of the play suggest that Shakespeare pencilled in a mother for Hero (he named her Innogen), but then removed her. Why should Shakespeare deprive these young women of their mothers?

Silences and outbursts

In a world of men, the women of Messina have two main options: to submit or to resist.

a Submission
    At first, Hero believes the prince woos her for himself. Then she is given to Claudio who subsequently rejects her. Finally, she is given a second time to the same man who had so cruelly spurned her. Script a discussion between a director and the actor playing Hero as they discuss how to give credibility to Hero's silence and compliance.

b Resistance
    Start with Beatrice's interruption of the messenger in 1.1, and list the times when she shows her independence and defiance. What sparks her off on each occasion?

Finding love in the world of Messina
Hero and Claudio
Their story shows the conventional rituals of aristocratic Elizabethan courtship and marriage – wooing by proxy, settlement of the dowry, formal betrothal, marriage ceremony.

Draw four columns. In the first column list each stage of the courtship and marriage of Hero and Claudio. In the second column write any thoughts you have about how conventional or spontaneous each stage of their courtship seems. Write Hero's feelings for Claudio in column three and, in column four, Claudio's for Hero. Do you think they find love?

Beatrice and Benedick

Most commentators on the play think that their story culminates in a 'marriage of true minds', a union of equals ('Man is not the measure of that which is human, but men and women are' Gerda Lerner).

a Some argue that the final kiss symbolises the love and harmony that Beatrice and Benedick have learned to share.

b Others think that the final kiss makes it clear that the voluble lady has finally had her mouth stopped.

Half the group collect evidence for **a** and the other half collect evidence for **b**. Debate the issue.

This is how the 1968 and 1982 RSC productions showed the moment when Beatrice and Benedick found love. How would *you* stage this moment?

Fashion

The Elizabethan aristocrat was a rich and glittering sight. Costumes for both sexes were extremely ornate and vastly expensive. The way you dressed was an indication of your rank and people were forbidden by law from wearing fabrics belonging to higher ranks. For example, Cloth of Gold, a material woven with pure gold threads (see 3.4.14–18), could only be worn by royalty and nobility.

Men's fashions

In the eyes of the traditionalists, men's fashions had become particularly effeminate by the end of the sixteenth century. Some noblemen wore make-up, had their hair curled at the barber's, smothered themselves in perfume, and wore single earrings and lovelocks (see picture opposite). This last fashion particularly angered the moralists of the day.

The fashionable English gallant also copied any foreign style that took his fancy. Such extremes in dress meant that the Englishman was often laughed at for his outrageous mixing of foreign fashions (see 3.2.24–30). The stylish combination for 1599 was German or Dutch trunk hose, French doublet, Spanish hat and Italian neckwear. Foreigners often commented on how frequently the English changed their fashions, particularly their hats, which 'ever changed with the next block' (1.1.56).

Such lavish ostentation made some Elizabethans very uneasy. They thought the aristocracy should be investing in their estates and not spending their wealth on clothes. Huge debts were accumulated as the nobility kept striving to outdo, or outdress, each other.

The fashionable aristocrat of 1599 (could this be Count Claudio?)

The Earl of Southampton was Shakespeare's patron. Shakespeare dedicated two long poems to him: *Venus and Adonis* and *The Rape of Lucrece*. Many believe that he may be the young man to whom Shakespeare addressed many of his sonnets.

This portrait of the earl, painted at about the time the play was

written, shows him dressed in the latest style. His doublet has very little padding (the heavily padded peascod doublet was beginning to go out of fashion) but his trunk hose are still very heavily padded.

Notice the expensive gloves, the ornate armour and the long lovelock trailing over his left shoulder.

'What a deformed thief this fashion is'

Costumes for both sexes distorted the natural human shape. The fashionable male peascod doublet was heavily padded in front to give the appearance of a large paunch. The male trunk hose (breeches) were also padded to accentuate this pear-shape. Women's costumes were even more extreme and uncomfortable (see page 88). Corsets formed tiny waists and stomachers flattened the breasts and abdomen. Clumsy metal farthingales ballooned the skirts into a huge bell-shape.

Much ado about appearance?

a Fashion words and pictures fill the play. How many fashion/appearance words can you find in the opening scene?

b From the information on pages 176 and 177, do you think Borachio was right to comment so cynically on Elizabethan fashions in 3.3?

c Read 3.2.1–54 and decide how much like a fashionable Elizabethan gallant Benedick has become. Suggest how the actor (and the other characters on stage) could highlight the changes.

d The Watch, being lower class, would wear very different clothes to the aristocrats. Design their costumes for an Elizabethan, Victorian or modern day production.

e Choose a character each and find out how many fashion words/images he or she uses during the course of the play.

f Find lines or words about fashion which help to convey the difficulty of knowing the difference between outward show and inner truth.

g Where in the play do dress and costume take on a serious and symbolic significance?

Kenneth Branagh said about his 1993 film of *Much Ado:* 'We consciously avoided setting this version in a specific time, but instead went for a look and an atmosphere that worked within itself, where clothes, props, architecture, language and customs all belong to the same timeless world. This imaginary world could exist anywhere along a continuum from 1700 to 1900.'

Try your hand at designing a costume for either Beatrice or Benedick that has a 'timeless' quality.

Mary 2nd. Daughter of
Sir Edward Fitton. Maid
of Honour to Queen Eliza
beth.

A portrait of Mary Fitton, maid of honour to Queen Elizabeth I, in all the splendour of the richest of Elizabethan costumes.

The language of the play

Talk, talk, talk!

People in Messina are always talking. At times their conversation is light, confident, quick and volatile. At times it is dark, heavy and intense, as events force people to confront the painful 'seeming truths' about themselves and those most dear to them. The language of the play is flexible and varied. There is clever repartee, good-natured teasing, pompous self-importance, friendly concern, but also taunts, cold malice, hurt anger, innocent bewilderment, grief and despair.

Shakespeare's prose

Only one third of the play is in verse. Two thirds are written in a fluid prose style that changes its qualities with each new character and situation. The range and flexibility of the prose in *Much Ado About Nothing* is remarkable.

Elegant politeness

Leonato, Don Pedro and the messenger set this tone in the opening scene (see pages 4 and 6). Each strives to outdo the other in elegantly phrased compliments and observations. Beatrice, of course, refuses to play this game! Talk together about how her interventions interrupt their pattern of polite phrases.

Good-natured wit and repartee

Don Pedro, Claudio and Benedick love to demonstrate their friendship in banter and teasing (see pages 12 and 14). But what do you think of their mockery in 5.1 and 5.4? Are they such close friends at the end of the play as they are at the start (see page 156)?

Rigid single-mindedness

Don John's speech is like a mask. He shows outward politeness (1.1.116) but conceals burning malice. His controlled hatred is expressed in the heavy and stiffly patterned prose of 1.3 (see page 20). Later it is concealed behind the concerned manner of his words in 3.2.59–100.

Attack and counter-attack
The sharpest encounters are between Beatrice and Benedick.
Remind yourself of their meetings leading up to the moment of crisis
in 2.1.181–216, where Benedick retires to lick his wounds. How
attractive and likeable do you find Beatrice at this point in the play?

Rambling incoherence
Dogberry's wandering sentences match his rambling brain. When he
is not studiously explaining why the Watch should have nothing to do
with criminals (3.3), he is failing to tell Leonato the vital information
that will avert the coming tragedy (3.5). When he is not botching the
cross-examination, he is smarting at being called an ass (4.2).

A kaleidoscope of speech

The prose varieties above are just a few of many. Find examples of
the following kinds of prose in the play:

- Young women talking together excitedly and irritably; a young
  woman flirting and making jokes with sexual undertones.
- Young men joking uneasily; drunken men speaking cynically; old
  men speaking disapprovingly to a young woman.
- A man choosing his words carefully so as not to offend his
  superior; a man offended by his superior but trying to hide it;
  a man attempting to speak impressively but being mockingly
  parodied.

Characters and language (in large groups)

Each person chooses a character from the play. Find two or three
lines which you think are typical of your character. Memorise them.
Then walk about the room as if you were that character. When you
meet someone, speak your lines to each other.

After you have spoken to everyone, go and stand with the people
you think are playing the same character as yourself (for example, if
you are a Don John, join up with others who sound like Don John).

Talk about what it was in the language that helped you to recognise
each other. Each character-group reports their findings to the rest.

Showing off with language – Classical allusions

Educated Elizabethans loved to display their learning and command of language. They would certainly have enjoyed the Classical allusions they heard as they watched a performance of *Much Ado About Nothing*:

> *Jove* was king of the gods in Roman mythology. When he travelled the earth in human disguise, Philemon, a poor peasant, gave him hospitality in his humble cottage (2.1.68–9). Jove was a habitual adulterer. To keep his sexual liaisons secret from his wife he adopted many disguises (for example, bull, satyr, swan), and was thus able to seduce many young women like Europa (5.4.43–51) and make them pregnant.

> *Troilus and Cressida* Troilus loved Cressida faithfully. She swore to be true to him, but proved faithless (5.2.24).

> *Hercules* was the ancient Greek strong-man. He performed many mighty physical tasks (the 'Labours of Hercules', 2.1.275) and numerous sexual ones too, such as impregnating all fifty daughters of the King of Thespis in one night! Cupid later punished him by making him the love-slave of Omphale, Queen of Lydia, who beat and ridiculed him, dressing herself in his armour while he was set to do the cooking, spinning and other female tasks (see 2.1.191).

Find out which characters make the allusions above. Decide why they do so (to impress, amuse, express fear, anger and so on). In which ways do the references to Jove, Hercules, Troilus and Cressida echo the different themes of the play?

Showing off their language – puns, word-play and repartee

Nearly everyone in Leonato's household enjoys playing with words, using the ambiguities of language to surprise, amuse and sometimes hurt.

- **Repartee** (witty retorts): see pages 8, 14, 90, 136
- **Puns** (playing with the meanings of words): see pages 38, 50, 86
- **Playing with ideas**: see pages 10, 28, 38
- **Sexual innuendoes**: see pages 28, 74, 146.

Showing off their language – malapropisms and mistaken meanings

Dogberry's attempts at fine speech leave the language in shreds. Malapropisms, misuse of words and mistaking of meanings are all found in his speech (see pages 78, 94, 120). The irony is that Dogberry succeeds in uncovering the truth where the cleverest people in Messina all fail!

The master-speakers of prose – Beatrice and Benedick

Most of what Beatrice and Benedick say is in prose. Their words reveal two very intelligent minds at work.

The language of their initial encounters (1.1 and 2.1) is aggressive and searching as each probes the other's defences. Yet beneath the mockery is a more complex relationship. As the play unfolds, both show a certain insecurity, a fear of either losing the other's respect (2.1.154–9) or admitting their own vulnerability (2.1.211–16).

Later, in 4.1, 5.2 and 5.4, Hero's dishonouring forces them to shed their defensive mockery. Here the prose they speak has the complexity and intensity of verse: a subtle and fluctuating meeting of minds (see page 116).

Take one of Benedick's prose soliloquies (2.1.154–9, 2.3.7–28 and 181–200). Compare it with Beatrice's soliloquy in 3.1.107–16.

List the different styles of prose that Beatrice and Benedick use. Put the lists side by side. At which point can their prose be described as a sympathetic exchange of ideas?

Racist language?

Characters refer unflatteringly in the play to Jews, Turks and Ethiops (2.3.212, 3.4.42, and 5.4.38). Do their remarks offend you? Would you accuse Shakespeare of racism, or defend him?

To cut or not to cut?

In the 1993 Kenneth Branagh film of *Much Ado*, Benedick's line 'This looks not like a nuptial' (Act 4 Scene 1, line 62) is cut. It comes just after the violent rejection of Hero by Claudio. Talk together about the gains and losses of cutting the line.

Shakespeare's blank verse

Although only one third of the play is written in blank (unrhymed) verse, it is spoken at significant moments and with powerful effect. There is nothing difficult about blank verse. Many believe it is based very closely on the natural rhythms of English speech.

Each line of blank verse has five alternating unstressed (x) and stressed (/) syllables (**iambic pentameter**), as in the first verse line of the play:

x / x / x / x / x /
'My liege, your highness may now do me good.' (1.1.216)

This rhythmic pattern and energy is frequently varied (but never completely lost), so that many different effects are created. Sometimes a line is shaped into two halves with a mid-line pause (**caesura**) and an end-of-line pause (**end-stopping**). Very often one line will 'flow' into the next (**enjambement** or run-on line).

Read the following examples aloud to hear some of these differences:
Claudio's farewell to Hero (4.1.93–101)
Leonato's grief (4.1.129–36)
the Friar's plan (4.1.203–36).

Sonnets, couplets and quatrains

Everyone laughs when Beatrice and Benedick's sonnets are produced at the end of the play. Many Elizabethan love sonnets had a rhyme scheme of three quatrains (ABAB/CDCD/EFEF) plus a final couplet (GG).

Does Beatrice speak part of a sonnet at the end of 3.1? Find other places in the play where characters speak in couplets or quatrains and decide why they do so.

The monument scene (5.3) is almost entirely in rhymed verse. What effect does this have?

Prose and verse

The men speak largely in prose when tricking Benedick (Act 2 Scene 3). The women speak entirely in verse when tricking Beatrice (Act 3 Scene 1). Suggest three possible reasons for the difference.

From prose to verse and from verse to prose

The fluid nature of the prose and verse in the play is further enhanced by the way in which characters frequently switch from one form to the other. Each transition has its own particular dramatic effect. For example, Claudio the romantic will lead Don Pedro into verse (1.1), while the bone-headed Dogberry remains stolidly in prose as all around him speak verse (5.1). The prose/verse transitions of 4.1 and 5.1 provide many clues as to the changes of tone and mood in these scenes.

Word pictures: in verse and prose

Beatrice's vivid word pictures are usually created in prose. Below is one student's response to Beatrice's 'God sends a curst cow short horns' (Act 2 Scene 1, line 18). Draw your own picture of one of the images in Beatrice's rare use of verse in Act 3 Scene 1, lines 107–16.

Planning and staging your production

Many beautiful sets have been designed for this play. One production had a bright mirror floor, a coppery glowing background and illuminated trees. As the curtain went up, music was heard, and shooting stars flashed across the sky. Cloaks, plumes and ribbons abounded. It was 'a delight to the senses'. At the close, Beatrice twirled Benedick around against the glow of a huge orange sun.

Yet this same set also hinted at darker strands in the play. Its mirrors and bright perspex showed privileged, self-indulgent people, all admiring their reflections. The reflecting surfaces emphasised how often characters noted each other as well as themselves. They also highlighted how rarely the characters saw the real image. The glittering set created an ambiguous world peopled with flippant men and women who cared little for emotions and sensitivities.

Draw the set

Below are the main features of the set for another production of *Much Ado About Nothing*. Use these clues to sketch, draw or model the set:

- set in a garden at the centre of a maze formed by yew hedges
- there is a chessboard formality to the layout of the garden
- one garden seat under the shadow of a hedge
- a seat can be lowered from above to swing to and fro
- there is a tree centre stage.

When you have completed your drawing/model, choose three scenes and work out how you would stage them on this set. Write a paragraph on how this set reflects some of the themes of the play.

Design your set and costumes

The play has been set in many different communities and historical periods: Restoration England, late nineteenth-century British India, a Middle American town in the 1890s, a 1930s cruise ship, a wealthy 1950s Mediterranean villa.

Design the set and costumes for your own production of the play. Illustrated histories of fashion and painting are helpful if you want to set it in a particular historical period or place.

Design your cast list

Designing your own cast list can greatly help your understanding. Turn to the list of characters on page 1. It groups the characters under Leonato's Household, The Military and The Town to help you see the structure of the play.

Draw up cast lists which rank the characters according to:

power and status   intelligence   common sense and capability
good-heartedness   dramatic importance   ability to deceive.

Produce a cast list for a feminist production (one that emphasises the women's point of view). Then write brief character sketches of the four lovers that this feminist production might put in its programme (about fifty words each).

Write your theatre programme notes

Research and prepare programme notes for your production of the play. Use the library and old theatre programmes. Here are some of the things that past performances of *Much Ado About Nothing* have included:

- Summary of the plot, the play's sources, dates of first productions.
- The Officers' Code: information about the nature of army life, the attitudes and beliefs of the officer class, masculine solidarity.
- Rank and Courtship: information on how social station plays an important part in shaping beliefs, attitudes to marriage and concern for reputation and honour.
- Details of past productions, comments from theatre critics, information on the actors, extracts from newspaper reviews.

Publicise your production

- Design a poster. It should make people eager to see your play.
- Design a flyer – a small handbill to advertise the production.
- Video a two-minute advertisement for your production.
- Work out a five-minute presentation to show potential sponsors.

Director's notes

Prepare a brief outline of the ideas in the play that you wish to emphasise in your production. Then focus on one scene in the play and prepare detailed notes on how you would highlight these ideas.

William Shakespeare 1564–1616

1564 Born Stratford-upon-Avon, eldest son of John and Mary Shakespeare.
1582 Married to Anne Hathaway of Shottery, near Stratford.
1583 Daughter, Susanna, born.
1585 Twins, son and daughter, Hamnet and Judith, born.
1592 First mention of Shakespeare in London. Robert Greene, another playwright, described Shakespeare as 'an upstart crow beautified with our feathers . . .'. Greene seems to have been jealous of Shakespeare. He mocked Shakespeare's name, calling him 'the only Shake-scene in a country' (presumably because Shakespeare was writing successful plays).
1595 A shareholder in 'The Lord Chamberlain's Men', an acting company that became extremely popular.
1596 Son Hamnet died, aged 11.
       Father, John, granted arms (acknowledged as a gentleman).
1597 Bought New Place, the grandest house in Stratford.
1598 Acted in Ben Jonson's *Every Man in His Humour*.
1599 Globe Theatre opens on Bankside. Performances in the open air.
1601 Father, John, dies.
1603 James I granted Shakespeare's company a royal patent: 'The Lord Chamberlain's Men' became 'The King's Men' and played about twelve performances each year at court.
1607 Daughter, Susanna, marries Dr John Hall.
1608 Mother, Mary, dies.
1609 'The King's Men' begin performing indoors at Blackfriars Theatre.
1610 Probably returned from London to live in Stratford.
1616 Daughter, Judith, marries Thomas Quiney.
       Died. Buried in Holy Trinity Church, Stratford-upon-Avon.

The plays and poems
(no one knows exactly when he wrote each play)

1589–1595 *The Two Gentlemen of Verona, The Taming of the Shrew, First, Second and Third Parts of King Henry VI, Titus Andronicus, King Richard III, The Comedy of Errors, Love's Labour's Lost, A Midsummer Night's Dream, Romeo and Juliet, King Richard II* (and the long poems *Venus and Adonis* and *The Rape of Lucrece*).

1596–1599 *King John, The Merchant of Venice, First and Second Parts of King Henry IV, The Merry Wives of Windsor, Much Ado About Nothing, King Henry V, Julius Caesar* (and probably the *Sonnets*).

1600–1605 *As You Like It, Hamlet, Twelfth Night, Troilus and Cressida, Measure for Measure, Othello, All's Well That Ends Well, Timon of Athens, King Lear.*

1606–1611 *Macbeth, Antony and Cleopatra, Pericles, Coriolanus, The Winter's Tale, Cymbeline, The Tempest.*

1613 *King Henry VIII, The Two Noble Kinsmen* (both probably with John Fletcher).

1623 Shakespeare's plays published as a collection (now called the First Folio).